ezra pound's
mauberley

ezra

pound's

mauberley

a study in composition

by john espey

Jenkins *,1913-*

811.3

university of california press
berkeley, los angeles, london

university of california press
berkeley and los angeles, california

university of california press, ltd.
london, england

first published 1955   LC* 54-6474
first paperback edition 1974
isbn: 0-520-02618-7
printed in the united states of america

hugh selwyn mauberley
from ezra pound *personae*.
copyright © 1926 by ezra pound
reprinted by permission of new directions publishing
corporation
and in england by permission of faber and faber limited

preface to
the paperback edition

Anyone interested in the genesis of this study can find an account of it in the *Proceedings of the Conference in the Study of Twentieth-Century Literature, Second Session* (East Lansing, May 3–5, 1962; pp. 113–115). My working title, *Some Notes on "Hugh Selwyn Mauberley"*, combined music with a degree of modesty, but the Editorial Committee of the University of California Press insisted on something fuller, and only a some-what formal heading finally earned approval. In the light of this, I was too timid to put forward my wife's suggestion for the title of Chapter 5: *Toujours Physique de l'Amour*.

When I was forced to re-read my own work a few years ago in order to comment on it in a bibliographical essay covering Pound scholarship that appeared in *Fifteen Modern American Authors* (Duke, 1969) I said:

John Espey's *Ezra Pound's Mauberley: A Study in Composition* attempted to trace in detail the materials that Pound had reshaped, following his own lead on the use of Gautier, and to base a reading on the implications of the poet's sources. From this distance, the author appears to draw a very long bow indeed in certain lines, but he is willing to stand his central ground, admitting that some pages seem to sound a faint note of (deliberate?) parody of the academic style. (For whatever its worth, Pound personally and generously insisted that only one serious error occurs in the book, adding, "But after all . . . you couldn't help it, you were born in the age of Freud," a remark that for him obviously settled the matter and for the author cut two ways.)

In a penetrating review of the book, Thomas Connolly (*Accent*, Winter 1956) insisted that the central question had not been resolved, quoting Pound himself as evidence against the critics who persisted in seeing any part of him in the poem after he had been "buried" in the opening stanzas. Connolly also added to the significance of the connection with Gourmont's work by drawing attention to specific verbal links with the "Translator's Note" following Pound's Englishing of *Physique de l'Amour*.

Recent years have brought little shift in position, though an evaluation of *Mauberley* has become a required part of any general discussion of Pound's earlier poetry.

The issue under discussion with Pound was the interpretation of the acron image in the first poem (see p. 80). I was then, as I am now, unconcerned with distinguishing between conscious and unconscious influences, but I have been told by persons in touch with Pound after his return to Italy that he came close to admitting some merit in what I had written on this point. In addition to Connolly's remarks on Gourmont, mention should be made of a recent note by Denis Donoghue in *Notes and Queries* (February 1970, pp. 49–50) that gives further support to the Jamesian themes of the poem with specific verbal connections with *The Awkward Age*.

In the text of the poem for this printing I have tried to reproduce all the sanctioned corrections and changes of later years. Here and there this may lead to slight confusion in interpreting my original commentary. For example, my effort to make something of the shift from "manifestation" to the plural (see p. 22) proved to be meaningless; the change was a compositor's error that rode through later printings uncorrected. And Pound in later years raised no objection to the silent correction of his Latin and his eccentric spelling of Browning's bishop (see p. 24). He also changed the sequence's subtitle (Life and Contacts) to (Contacts and Life) in 1957, apparently wishing to emphasize the division of the poem between Mauberley's contacts and life in the first section, and his more objective presentation in the second.

For the rest, I would repeat my warning (see p. 101) against reading what I have written as a substitute for the poem itself. And I should like to thank not only all those who have corresponded with me about my reading of *Mauberley* but also those editors of anthologies who have given me credit in their batteries of notes as well as those who have not.

preface

This study, stemming almost accidentally from a few casual discoveries, grew into an experiment in criticism, focused on the question of how effective the traditional academic method of attack, with its full panoply of textual collation, identification of sources, and historical method, would prove when used in analysing a piece of contemporary poetry. That the body of Ezra Pound's work submits itself more fruitfully than that of many other writers to such an approach is, I think, obvious. At the same time, I should like to think that such insights into *Mauberley* as these explorations provide are indications of a method that could be profitably used elsewhere. I should like to think, too, that at least a few parts of the study indicate the classic attack's flexibility and show that it need not be a fixed strategy followed without consideration of its subject's nature.

At many points I have called on my colleagues at the University of California at Los Angeles for help, and I wish to thank Frederick M. Carey for his patience in answering what must often have seemed to him alarmingly elementary questions on the classics; Hugh G. Dick for suggesting possible originals for some portraits in *Mauberley*; Majl Ewing for his generosity in finding and giving me a copy of the first issue of *Poetical Works of Lionel Johnson*; Blake Nevius for criticizing the manuscript during composition and saving me from many errors; Richard Rudolph and Howard Hibbett, Jr., for their aid on Sino-Japanese names; Arnold Schwab for information on the family of Sir Max Beerbohm; and John Stafford, now of Brooklyn College, for sharing an office with me without visible annoyance during the greater part of my research. Without the help of all these persons this study would lack a number of whatever merits it now has; but the study would never have been seriously undertaken originally, much less completed, without the sustained interest of James E. Phillips, Jr., and my major debt is to him for his consistent willingness to listen, read, and criticize, and for his astutely timed refreshment.

I wish also to thank Glenn Gosling, of the University of California Press, for his expeditious handling of the manuscript; and his colleague, James Kubeck, for his painstaking editorial work.

The Ezra Pound material in the Department of Special Collections of the Library of the University of California at Los Angeles, gathered under the stimulus of the Librarian, Lawrence Clark Powell, has been of great help to me.

For permission to quote copyrighted material I wish to express my thanks to: George Allen and Unwin, Ltd. for *Ernest Dowson*, by Victor Plarr, published by Elkin Mathews (copyright, 1914); Appleton-Century-Crofts for *Modern Poetry*, edited by Kimon Friar and John Malcolm Brinnin (copyright, 1951); Les Belles Lettres for *Bucoliques grecs*, edited by P. E. Legrand (copyright, 1927); Chatto and Windus, and George W. Stewart for *New Bearings in English Poetry*, by F. R. Leavis (copyright, 1932); J. M. Dent and Sons, Ltd. for *Victory*, by Joseph Conrad (copyright, 1915); Faber and Faber, Ltd. for *Selected Poems of Ezra Pound*, edited by T. S. Eliot (copyright, 1928); Harcourt, Brace and Company, Inc. for *Language as Gesture*, by R. P. Blackmur (copyright, 1953); Harcourt Brace and Company, Inc. and Faber and Faber Ltd. for *The Letters of Ezra*

Pound, edited by D. D. Paige (copyright, 1952); Oxford University Press for *The Notebooks of Henry James*, edited by F. O. Matthiessen and Kenneth B. Murdock (copyright, 1947), and *Jules Laforgue and the Ironic Inheritance*, by Warren Ramsey (copyright, 1953); Pearn, Pollinger and Higham, Ltd. for *Aspects of Modern Poetry*, by Edith Sitwell (copyright, 1934); the editors of *Poetry* for early articles and reviews by Ezra Pound and Virgil Geddes; and Henry Regnery Company for *Achievement in American Poetry*, by Louise Bogan (copyright, 1951).

The principal body of Ezra Pound's poetry is available in *Personæ* and *The Cantos*, both of which volumes are published in the United States by New Directions, and in Great Britain by Faber and Faber Ltd.

J.J.E.

contents

I unresolved canon

Few modern poems have received more notice than Ezra Pound's *Hugh Selwyn Mauberley*,* but anyone examining the body of criticism centered on this sequence is struck by the variety of readings it has received and the continuing disagreement on three important points. The first of these is the relationship between Ezra Pound himself and Hugh Selwyn Mauberley, whether the two are to be identified wholly or in part or not at all; the second is the question of the poem's construction, whether it is a series of almost unrelated pieces arbitrarily patched together or a strictly balanced composition or something between the two; and the third is the nature of the poem's ultimate base, if indeed one can assume that such a base exists.

Equally apparent as the prevailing disagreement on these points—as well as the oppressively solemn tone of much contemporary criticism—is the possibility of following at least one approach that has gone largely unexplored. That the poem has never been subjected to detailed scrutiny in relation to the materials from which Pound shaped it may be a result of Pound's own annoyance with anything resembling the officially academic. But

---

* The text of *Hugh Selwyn Mauberley* appears on pp. 117–133.

his own prose works and the recent publication of both *The Letters of Ezra Pound* and some of Pound's notes on *Mauberley* in Friar and Brinnin's *Modern Poetry* offer too many tempting leads to be ignored. Consequently, much of what follows falls under the head of "source-hunting." That the tracing of a source may substitute an appearance of understanding for genuine penetration is perfectly possible, but so long as one distinguishes between the casual source—the discovery of which is a harmless enough pastime—and the source that genuinely informs a piece of writing, the method has its own objective values. For an artist of the order of Pound, himself so frequently the PH.D. *manqué* in both prose and poetry, it can prove peculiarly revealing.

To give greater immediate coherence and to provide a groundwork for the individual studies that follow, none of which insures a systematic and full discussion of the poem from beginning to end, some outline of the sequence is necessary. I would say, then, that in *Mauberley* Pound, modeling his verse on the rhythms of Gautier and Bion, and working from a surface of the French poets whose work he had already assimilated but had recently reread for his *Little Review* article "A Study in French Poets" (February, 1918), uses a foundation of his own experience for the poem, interpreting it through attitudes revealed in his recent "Baedekers" of Henry James (*Little Review*, August and September, 1918)[1] and Remy de Gourmont (*Little Review*, February–March, 1919), the latter reinforcing his earlier remarks on Gourmont (*Fortnightly Review*, December 1, 1915; *Poetry*, January, 1916); and that Pound creates in the person of Hugh Selwyn Mauberley, who appears only in the latter half of the poem and in contrast to Pound himself, a mask of the contemporary aesthete to show what the minor artist could expect from the England of the day. The entire suite rehandles the theme Pound had used in *Homage to Sextus Propertius*, in which, taking

---

[1] Both the *Instigations* and *Make it New* texts of the James essay fail to show that the section on *The Middle Years* originally appeared in *The Egoist* (January, 1918).

certain passages from the Latin elegist's work, he had created a poem concerned with the poet's place in a society that ignored private strength and passion in favor of assumed public rectitude and morality.

Tracing the movement of *Hugh Selwyn Mauberley* very briefly: it opens with an ironic "*Ode*" on Ezra Pound himself, in which, using the clichés of the time and of his critics, he actually reveals his own character and career. Then, moving on to the age in which he lives, Pound characterizes it in his own voice (II), exposing those forces that make the artist's full realization impossible in modern England, the "tawdry cheapness" (III) brought about by commercialism and the insistence on money as an aesthetic standard, the degradation of literature by the pandering of the press, the self-corrupting trend in democracy that bankrupts society. The climax of this denunciation is reached in the First World War with its sacrifice of youth (IV) going down to death for the sake of a diseased tradition (V). Turning from the present, Pound traces the sources of this degeneration, beginning with the overpowering of aesthetic values in the pre-Raphaelite period by the official morality of Gladstone and Ruskin (*Yeux Glauques*), followed by the Nineties ("*Siena Mi Fé; Disfecemi Maremma*"), when the artist was so driven that he took refuge in collapse or mediocrity. The list of Pound's (and, by implication, Mauberley's) "contacts" in the contemporary world follows, each portrait an illustration of what either yielding to, or resisting, the age's demands means in personal terms. The Jew (*Brennbaum*) erases all his inherited traditions in the interests of elegant conformity and acceptance; the opportunist author (*Mr. Nixon*) sucks up to the journals for the sake of popular success; the dedicated and uncompromising stylist (X) scrapes along in a collapsing country cottage; and the educated woman (XI) becomes the inheritor of sterile traditions that she does not understand. Inspecting himself in relation to the fashionable literary circles of London (XII), Pound realizes that he is unacceptable on all counts, and bows out with a brilliant, derivative love lyric (*Envoi*) that combines echoes of many standard British poets and controverts the surface judgments of his critics used in the opening *Ode*.

In the second section of the sequence, Hugh Selwyn Mauberley emerges as an individual for the first time. Each of the poems opens with a seeming parallel drawn from the first section, but develops it in thematic opposition. Mauberley's limits as an artist are displayed (*Mauberley*); his tardy realization that life may have had something to offer him through active passion is explored (II); his inability to conform to the age ("*The Age Demanded*") is revealed, leading into subjective reveries that finally engulf him as he drifts on to his death (IV), leaving behind only one work (*Medallion*), in which the scene of the *Envoi* is rehandled with unconsciously ironic emphasis on bookish precision lacking any awareness of invitation and passion.

This reading, which in many parts is indebted to F. R. Leavis, Edith Sitwell, and Hugh Kenner, moves from Pound (*Ode*—V) through Pound's and Mauberley's contacts (*Yeux Glauques*—XII) to the disappearance of Pound (*Envoi*) and the independent emergence of Mauberley (*Mauberley*—III), with Pound acting now, at least on the surface, only as tolerant observer, and concludes with Mauberley's single poem (*Medallion*). It presents Pound first, then the two poets in their overlapping areas, and finally, as the first leaves to survive—just as Pound was soon to leave London for Paris—the second remains and goes passively to his death. The most important original features of this reading are its insistence on a complete divorce between Pound and Mauberley so far as the sequence itself is concerned, and an equal insistence on the balanced structure of the work as a whole. That a tone of ribaldry underlies Pound's "tolerance" in the second section, and that the entire suite is grounded on a definite base, I shall attempt to demonstrate later.

If at first glance this reading seems thoroughly arbitrary and dogmatic, it is at least a reading that a considerable body of evidence can be used to support, and one can open that evidence with what may seem to be an absurdly pedantic exercise: the collating of some *Mauberley* texts and tables of contents.

Hugh Selwyn Mauberley was first printed in 1920 by the Ovid Press in England, and the table of contents read:

MAUBERLEY

CONTENTS

Part I.

The table of contents for the first American appearance of
the full suite in *Poems 1918–21*, published by Boni and
Liveright in 1921, is the same with the exception of Part II,
which appeared as

Part II.

(Mauberley)

I.

II.

"The age demanded"

IV.

Medallion

The most interesting point here is that neither table of contents
gives a hint that the opening *Ode* is Ezra Pound's ode.[2] Only in

---

[2] In *The Dial* for September, 1920, the first six poems of *Mauberley*
(*Ode-Yeux Glauques*) were reprinted from the Ovid Press text. This
truncated version is of no importance for the poem itself but it may have
had an effect on its critical history. The six poems were published under
the title "H. S. Mauberly," the epigraph and "Life and Contacts"
omitted, and the first poem was titled simply "Ode pour l'élection de
son sépulchre." In addition to the misspelling "Mauberly" the text
reads "A bright Apollo" for "O bright Apollo" and "cartoons" for
"cartons." Readers of this version, ending as it does with *Yeux Glauques*,
would be led to think that *Mauberley* as a unit is far more strongly pre-
Raphaelite in emphasis than it is. Thus Yvor Winters always stresses the
pre-Raphaelite and Nineties elements in the poem, without apparently
recognizing the contemporary portraits, and accuses Pound of both
yearning for and satirizing both periods' mediocre aspects. (See, for
example, *In Defense of Reason*, p. 68, where the title is given as *Hugh
Selwyn Mauberly*.) The same emphasis had appeared earlier (*Hound and
Horn*, April–June, 1933, p. 538.) in Winters' comment: "Pound writes
a lugubrious lament for the passing of pre-Raphaelitism, yet deliberately
makes pre-Raphaelitism (and himself) appear ludicrous."

In the light of *The Dial*'s use of part of *Mauberley* in 1920 and Boni
and Liveright's publication of the whole in 1921, it is difficult to sup-
port Louise Bogan throughout when she writes in *Achievement in
American Poetry 1900–1950*: "Pound's 'Hugh Selwyn Mauberly'"

the text of the Ovid Press edition is the first poem titled

E. P.
ODE POUR L'ÉLECTION DE SON SEPULCHRE
I

The Boni and Liveright edition omits "E. P." even here, and the sequence opens with

ODE POUR L'ELECTION DE SON
SEPULCHRE
I

The omission of "E. P." in both tables of contents and in one text is probably one reason for a number of critics' making a complete identification of Pound and Mauberley. As it stands, the Boni and Liveright edition indicates nowhere that Pound dominates the first part and Mauberley the second, except for the parenthetical heading under Part II.

But a further, and equally misleading, confusion has resulted from these first two printings. The table of contents in each makes clear that the *Ode* as such is simply the first poem. This is important, for the *Ode* has become almost a standard anthology piece in recent years, often printed, however, as if it were made up of the first poem plus II, III, IV, and V. Yet if one were to

---

[*sic*] (1920) presents a concentrated survey of Pound's London career as well as a dire criticism of postwar life. Written with comparative straightforwardness in stanzas brilliantly compressed, Mauberly appears as a minor poet who is Pound and yet not Pound and who turns, at the end, toward some refuge in the tropic seas. Pound himself was about to leave London for Paris, and finally, in 1925, for Rapallo, where he was to spend a long series of increasingly embittered and obsessive years. 'Mauberly,' not published in America until 1926 (in *Personæ*) had a belated influence upon American writing." Pound spent the first months of 1923 in Rapallo, returned to Paris for a time, and settled permanently in Italy in 1924.

follow this through, there is nothing to keep one from going right on to XII; for the numerals are omitted only when Pound gives an individual section its own title, and they carry to the end of the entire first part. This is clear in the Ovid Press listing of Part II, where the third and fifth poems are given both numerals and titles. All of this becomes genuinely useful when one realizes that the *Ode*, written ironically in the third person as the age's judgment of Pound, ends with his literary death when he "passed from men's memory in *l'an trentuniesme de son eage*." This particular shade of irony, probably derived from Villon as the quotation would indicate, ends with this poem, and the next one introduces with fine dramatic effect the voice of the man who has just been so condescendingly dismissed, a voice that renders in characteristic tones a judgment on the age, and a voice that holds throughout the first section.

This is partly clarified by the arrangement of the text in *Personæ* (Horace Liveright, 1926), where the opening title and numeral are reversed to read

I

E. P. ODE POUR L'ELECTION DE SON
SEPULCHRE

but it is not until the *Selected Poems* (New Directions, 1949) that the ambiguity is eliminated by simply opening the first part with

E. P. ODE POUR L'ELECTION DE SON SEPULCHRE

Thus both the anthologists and the critics have been misled at times by the early texts into seeing the first five poems as a more distinct unit within the section than they actually form, and some critics have attempted to carry over the *Ode*'s ironic tone into passages where irony may indeed function, but not in the manner of the *Ode* proper.

With this distinction, and with the basic division of the sequence, established, many problems automatically disappear.

The separation of Ezra Pound from Hugh Selwyn Mauberley[3] becomes apparent; the restatements in the "Mauberley"[4] section of phrases from the opening poems begin to look more like thematic variants than direct extensions; and a certain balance—even a logical structure—shows in the ordering of what has more than once been called a series of disconnected fragments. Even a typographical contrast emphasizes the division, with the use of the Greek alphabet in the first section's Greek quotations and tags as against the transliteration of Greek into the Roman alphabet in the second's.

A more detailed examination of the texts reveals Pound's revisions, interesting in themselves and indicative of both his method and his personal hand in certain editions. Thus the lines that now read

> But a tawdry cheapness
> Shall outlast our days.

originally stood as

> But a tawdry cheapness
> Shall reign throughout our days.

---

[3] Judgments like F. R. Leavis' in *New Bearings in English Literature*, characterizing all of *Mauberley* as "the summing-up of an individual life" and "quintessential autobiography," finding in the poem "a recognition of bankruptcy, of a devoted life summed up in futility," appear dubious once the division of the poem is clear, as does Edith Sitwell's statement in *Aspects of Modern Poetry* that the second part of *Mauberley* is "a quintessence of the poems which precede it." Virgil Geddes, writing in *Poetry* (November, 1922), said much the same thing when, commenting on the second poem of the "Mauberley" section, he wrote: "And this, half humorously, half cynically, gives his [Pound's] present mood toward his art. . . . Here is the final deduction, the proposed estimate, the elevated résumé, without the enumeration of uninteresting activities. The synthesis without the catalogue."

[4] Following custom, I refer to the entire sequence as *Hugh Selwyn Mauberley* or *Mauberley*, but in an effort to avoid confusion I refer to the individual himself as Hugh Selwyn Mauberley or Mauberley, and to the second part of the suite as the "Mauberley" section.

Here the revision, which first appeared in the 1921 text, is in the interests of compactness and stronger statement. The same text contains two other revisions. In the second poem of the "Mauberley" section, the lines that now read

> —Given that is his "fundamental passion,"
> This urge to convey the relation
> Of eye-lid and cheek-bone
> By verbal manifestations;

originally read

> Given, that is, his urge
> To convey the relation
> Of eye-lid and cheek-bone
> By verbal manifestation;

in which the revisions are apparently made in favor of the cliché and the blurring of an exact rhyme. In the same poem, "irides" has replaced the original "irises," probably to emphasize its use as a double image for both flower (in contrast to "orchid") and eye, with the revised reading giving greater weight to the eye and indicating the final use of the figure as it affects the closing *Medallion*.

Pound's hand in the 1926 *Personæ* text is shown by the first appearance of the "Mauberley" section's separate epigraph, drawn from Ovid (*Metamorphoses*, VII, 786), which reads in all subsequent texts just as it does in 1926:

> "*Vacuos exercet aera morsus.*"

The addition of the epigraph, untranslatable though it is without the preposition *in* before *aera*, is plainly an effort to clarify the concluding stanza of the second "Mauberley" poem:

> Mouths biting empty air,
> The still stone dogs,
> Caught in metamorphosis, were
> Left him as epilogues.

With the publication of the 1949 *Selected Poems*, further changes occur. The covering epigraph from Nemesianus—*Vocat aestus in umbram*—has disappeared; possibly, though not very probably, because more than one annotator in the anthologies had chosen to render *aestus* as *aestas*, translating it as "summer" instead of "heat"; and the subtitle "(Life and Contacts)" has also gone, together with the 1926 note:

The sequence is so distinctly a farewell to London that the reader who chooses to regard this as an exclusively American edition may as well omit it and turn at once to page 205.

These deletions seem to be indications of the relative unimportance of the original epigraph and subtitle.

Beyond these points, the most notable aspect of the text's successive states is the slow tidying up of the 1920 edition's more conspicuous errors. The Ruskin title in *Yeux Glauques* (derived from "Of Kings' Treasuries," the opening lecture in *Sesame and Lilies*) reads "Kings Treasuries" in 1920, gets home quickly with "Kings' Treasuries" in 1921, and then unaccountably falls off in 1926 to "King's Treasuries." In *Mr. Nixon* the name "Bloughram" stands thus in the 1920 text and all the American texts; only in the 1948 Faber and Faber reprint of the 1928 Faber and Gwyer *Selected Poems*, with T. S. Eliot's introduction, does it read "Blougram." In the eleventh poem of the first section, "Milésien" of the opening line is repeated exactly in the fifth line in 1920. The 1921 reading of the repetition is "Milésian," which is repeated in 1926, and not until 1949 do we get "Milesian," which Pound presumably wants as the English form in contrast to the French. To conclude this catalogue, the "neo-Nietzschean" of the present text rode through 1920 and 1921 as "neo-Neitzschean."

Although these points are of very little individual importance, taken together they do indicate that the process may not yet be completed; that one need not be bound by the rendering of Ovid quoted above, the dropping of the preposition being almost certainly accidental. They also indicate that one has the right to look with some suspicion at "Jaquemart," which looks as if it should be "Jacquemart," at "Gallifet," which looks as if it should be "Galliffet," and at "ΝΥΚΤΙΣ ᾽ΑΓΑΛΜΑ," which looks as if it should be "ΝΥΚΤΟΣ ᾽᾽ΑΓΑΛΜΑ"—all three readings unchanged from 1920 to 1949—especially if their sources can be established. A search for *le mot juste* obviously does not always lead directly to *l'orthographe exacte*.

A study of the shifting accents and letters in the fifteen Greek words of *Mauberley*'s first section is a curiosity in its own right, but the real sport here is to be found among the anthologists and is no part of this study. If the text of *Mauberley* that follows these pages is altogether accurate in this respect, it flouts a tradition of over thirty years' standing. This is a minor matter, of course, but if an examination of the more important texts can establish a number of valuable points for a reading of *Mauberley*, it is perhaps not too optimistic to hope that further analysis may yield further insights.

[Since this was written, Mr. Pound has sanctioned four changes in *Hugh Selwyn Mauberley*, and they have been incorporated in the text printed with this study. He does not accept any alteration in the Latin epigraph of the "Mauberley" section, or any change in the spelling of "Bloughram."—J.J.E.]

2 émaux et camées (or the bay state hymn book)

In *Criterion* for July, 1932, Ezra Pound, in the course of a memorial comment on Harold Monro, took time out for an aside:

> [Mr Eliot] displayed great tact, or enjoyed good fortune, in arriving in London at a particular date with a formed style of his own. He also participated in a movement to which no name has ever been given.
>
> That is to say, at a particular date in a particular room, two authors, neither engaged in picking the other's pocket, decided that the dilutation of *vers libre*, Amygism, Lee Masterism, general floppiness had gone too far and that some counter-current must be set going. Parallel situation centuries ago in China. Remedy prescribed 'Émaux et Camées' (or the Bay State Hymn Book). Rhyme and regular strophes.
>
> Results: Poems in Mr Eliot's *second* volume, not contained in his first ('Prufrock', *Egoist*, 1917), also 'H. S. Mauberley'.
>
> Divergence later.

That the relationship between *Émaux et Camées* and *Hugh Selwyn Mauberley* has never been fully explored may be a result of the greater respectability among the critics of Eliot's work as against Pound's, and the fact that the direct influence of Gautier on Eliot's 1920 volume is not actually very strong. That is, what influence exists *is* largely (though by no means entirely) a matter of "rhyme and regular strophes."

The relation between Pound and Gautier,[5] however, exists on quite other levels and serves to emphasize the academic traditionalism of Pound's taste as well as his separation by at least a full literary generation from Eliot. Sir Arthur Quiller-Couch, thinking it "no insult to include any English poet, born in our time, under the great name 'Victorian,'" included Pound's *Portrait* and *Ballad for Gloom* in *The Oxford Book of Victorian Verse*, and the two poems rest comfortably in its pages. Pound's much publicized rejection of Milton has tended to obscure the largely standard pattern of his enthusiasms: the Greek and Latin poets (with certain individual reservations), Dante and Cavalcanti, Chaucer, Shakespeare, Browning, Landor, and Beddoes. He holds FitzGerald's *Rubaiyat*, the poems of Dowson and Lionel Johnson in higher esteem than do most of his own or Eliot's contemporaries. His interest in Gautier is a part of this pattern and Gautier has been one of his immediate teachers. Writing to Iris Barry in 1916, Pound advised:

Theophile Gautier is, I suppose, the next man who can write. Perfectly plain statements like his "Carmen est maigre" should teach one a number of things. His early poems are many of them no further advanced than the Nineties. Or to put it more fairly the English Nineties got about as far as Gautier had got in 1830, and before he wrote "L'Hippopotame".

---

[5] Babette Deutsch briefly notes the influence of Gautier upon *Mauberley* (*Poetry in Our Time*, pp. 129–130), and René Taupin draws some direct parallels between *Émaux et Camées* and *Mauberley* in *L'Influence du symbolisme français sur la poésie américaine* (pp. 155–156).

A number of years later (1928) he wrote to René Taupin, then gathering material for his *L'Influence du symbolisme français sur la poésie américaine*: "Gautier j'ai etudié et je le révère."

The first unmistakable echoes of Gautier in Pound's work occur in *Lustra* (1915), specifically in two poems, *Albâtre* and *To a Friend Writing on Cabaret Dancers*. The first of these is an added note for Gautier's *Symphonie en Blanc Majeur*:

> This lady in the white bath-robe which she calls a peignoir,
> Is, for the time being, the mistress of my friend,
> And the delicate white feet of her little white dog
> Are not more delicate than she is,
> Nor would Gautier himself have despised their contrasts
>   in whiteness
> As she sits in the great chair
> Between the two indolent candles.

Here the surface is obvious enough, but in the second poem, the use of Gautier enters in other ways, some quite as apparent, as in the use of quotation, but others less so, as in the incorporation of vocabulary:

> And so Pepita
> Flares on the crowded stage before our tables
> Or slithers about between the dishonest waiters—
>   "CARMEN EST MAIGRE, UN TRAIT DE
>   BISTRE
>   CERNE SON ŒIL DE GITANA"
> And "rend la flamme",
>   you know the deathless verses.
> I search the features, the avaricious features
> Pulled by the kohl and rouge out of resemblance—
> Six pence the object for a change of passion.

Here the opening lines of Gautier's *Carmen* and the later phrase from the poem tend to conceal another echo of Gautier—and of *Émaux et Camées*—from another poem, *Coquetterie Posthume*, which opens

Quand je mourrai, que l'on me mette,
Avant de clouer mon cercueil,
Un peu de rouge à la pommette,
Un peu de noir au bord de l'œil.

Car je veux, dans ma bière close,
Comme le soir de son aveu,
Rester éternellement rose,
Avec du kh'ol sous mon œil bleu.

A possible additional echo occurs at the end of Pound's poem
with

Night after night,
No change, no change of program, "*Che!*
"*La donna è mobile.*"

which should be set beside the next to the last stanza of *Les
Joujoux de la Morte*:

Et des pleurs vous mouillent la joue
Quand *la Donna è mobile*,
Sur le rouleau qui tourne et joue,
Expire avec un son filé.

The evidence here should not be pressed, nor can one make any
useful judgment of the level, conscious or unconscious, on which
Pound is using "the kohl and the rouge" or the title of what is,
after all, an obvious enough song to refer to. But at least Pound's
immersion in *Émaux et Camées* is apparent as he begins to take
over Gautier's vocabulary, his method of flat statement, and his
general frame of reference.

Further evidence of this immersion appears in *Poems 1918–
21*, the greater part of which is taken up by *Homage to Sextus
Propertius* and *Hugh Selwyn Mauberley*, but which also contains
Langue d'Oc with its supplementary section *Moeurs Contem-*

poraines, a title derived from Remy de Gourmont.[6] Here one sees, most conspicuously, Pound's eagerness to incorporate Gautier's method, as Taupin has pointed out, in such passages as

> At a friend of my wife's there is a photograph,
> A faded, pale brownish photograph,
> Of the times when the sleeves were large,
> Silk, stiff and large above the *lacertus,*
> That is, the upper arm,
> And décolleté. ...
>   It is a lady,
> She sits at a harp,
> Playing.

There is another connection with Gautier here, a more immediate one, though at the same time a less important one, perhaps; for the title of this fifth section of *Moeurs Contemporaines* is "*Nodier raconte* ..." The unwary reader may assume this to be a simple reference to Charles Nodier, but it is actually the opening phrase of *Inès de las Sierras,* itself drawn from Nodier's book of the same title, and a poem that exhibits in its second stanza a pair of "international" rhymes as ambitious as any attempted by Eliot or Pound:

> Nodier raconte qu'en Espagne
> Trois officiers cherchant un soir
> Une venta dans la campagne,
> Ne trouvèrent qu'un vieux manoir;
>
> Un vrai château d'Anne Radcliffe,
> Aux plafonds que le temps ploya,
> Aux vitraux rayés par la griffe
> Des chauves-souris de Goya.

---

[6] "Il n'y a de livres que ceux où un écrivain s'est raconté lui-meme en racontant les mœurs de ses contemporains—leurs rêves, leurs vanités, leurs amours, et leurs folies." Pound had first used this as epigraph for his review of Eliot's *Prufrock* (*Poetry*, August, 1917). Gourmont is writing of Flaubert.

In *Moeurs Contemporaines*, as in *Cabaret Dancers*, the most interesting observation is the completeness with which Pound fastens upon *Émaux et Camées*, taking up phrases and using whatever comes to hand, often quite outside the original context. The "kohl and rouge" come from a poem in which Gautier gives directions for his own laying out; the poem in which *La Donna è mobile* is mentioned trembles with the same minor pathos that infuses Eugene Field's *Little Boy Blue*, the tune being one played by the music box of a little dead girl whose coffin is no larger than a violin case; and the relationship between the opening of *Inès de las Sierras* and the fifth section of *Moeurs Contemporaines* is an indication of nothing more than that Pound, like the nineteenth-century French traveler, is setting down the significant details of what he has seen. At the same time, the influence of Gautier is so pervasive here that even though *Émaux et Camées* is only one source of *Hugh Selwyn Mauberley*, the use to which Pound puts his model is worth examining on more than one level.

Pound's reasons for turning to *Émaux et Camées* are probably clear enough from the *Criterion* quotation already cited. In addition to this, however, it is worth noting that he contributed a short article, "The Hard and the Soft in French Poetry," to the February, 1918 issue of *Poetry*, in which he spoke of Gautier as a "hard" poet as opposed to a "soft" poet like Samain. He drew the same distinction in his *Little Review* survey of the same month, "A Study in French Poets," and from the use of the medallion and engraver themes in *Mauberley* he probably had in mind Gautier's own statement of the purpose of *Émaux et Camées*, which Gautier had made in his essay "Les Progrès de la Poésie Française depuis 1830":

Ce titre, *Émaux et Camées*, exprime le dessein de traiter sous forme restreinte de petits sujets, tantôt sur plaque d'or ou de cuivre avec les vives couleurs de l'émail, tantôt avec la roue du graveur de pierres fines, sur l'agate, la cornaline ou l'onyx. Chaque pièce devait être un médaillon à enchâsser sur le couvercle d'un coffret, un cachet à porter au doigt, serti dans un bague, quelque chose qui rappelât les empreintes de médailles antiques qu'on voit chez les peintres et les sculpteurs.

Mauberley contains two quotations from *Émaux et Camées*, though only one of them is by Gautier. The twelfth poem of the first section opens with

> "Daphne with her thighs in bark
> "Stretches toward me her leafy hands,"—
> Subjectively.

In his notes on *Mauberley*, Kimon Friar writes: "Pound wrote the editor that this is a translation, but does not say from whom." The lines come from *Le Château du Souvenir*:

> Un jour louche et douteux se glisse
> Aux vitres jaunes du salon
> Où figurent, en haute lisse,
> Les aventures d'Apollon.
>
> Daphné, les hanches dans l'écorce,
> Étend toujours ses doigts touffus;
> Mais aux bras du dieu qui la force
> Elle s'éteint, spectre confus.

Pound has characteristically taken the two lines and put them to his own use. Daphne is no longer a figure in the salon's décor, but becomes indeed the laurel with which the poet is crowning himself. The lines are an example, not particularly striking, of Pound's ability as a translator—more precisely, here, of his knack for fitting a quotation to his own purpose with the substitution of "toward me" for "toujours."

The other quotation, if it can be called that, comes at the beginning of the "Mauberley" section:

> Turned from the "eau-forte
> Par Jaquemart"
> To the strait head
> Of Messalina:

Although, for the surface of the poem, the text is perfectly intelligible, with Mauberley turning away from the detailed etching to the severe medallion, the lines acquire more specific meaning if one has at hand the edition of *Émaux et Camées* published by Charpentier. Its title page reads in part:

THÉOPHILE GAUTIER

ÉMAUX

ET

CAMÉES

ÉDITION DÉFINITIVE

AVEC UNE EAU-FORTE PAR J. JACQUEMART

Facing this, and enclosed in a medallionlike border, is the etching itself, showing Gautier in three-quarter face, a portrait that looks not altogether unlike a weightier and more bravely bearded version of Pound's photograph by Alvin Langdon Coburn that serves as frontispiece to *Lustra*. "Jaquemart" is clearly a casual error that has ridden unnoticed through successive editions, like "Bloughram," of which Pound wrote to Friar, "reference to Browning's bishop, allegoric," thus requiring correction to "Blougram" and eliminating all ingenious speculation on the possibility of a Joycean portmanteau cross of Blougram and Brougham. [But see the note at the end of the preceding section.]

But when Pound wrote to Friar that the title of the sixth poem in the first section, *Yeux Glauques*, was not a quotation, one suspects the accuracy of his memory or feels his annoyance at the scholarly pursuit of these details. For *Yeux Glauques* is both quotation and translation from *Émaux et Camées*, and the poem from which it is taken echoes through much of this particular poem in *Mauberley*. Gautier's phrase, which is also the title of his poem, is *Cærulei Oculi*, and Pound's adaptation of the Latin is itself derived from the poem's second stanza; the first stanza and many other lines are reflected in Pound's description of the pre-Raphaelite Muse, whom he uses to focus his portrait of the period. *Cærulei Oculi* opens

> Une femme mystérieuse,
> Dont la beauté trouble mes sens,
> Se tient debout, silencieuse,
> Au bord des flots retentissants.
>
> Ses yeux, où le ciel se reflète,
> Mêlent à leur azur amer,
> Qu'étoile une humide paillette,
> Les teintes glauques de la mer.

It is perhaps worth noting in passing that "glauque" is a favorite word with Gautier, not only in his poems—"Le manteau glauque de la mer" (*Les Néréides*); "le glauque rideau" (*Le Château du Souvenir*)—but also in his prose. In *Mademoiselle de Maupin* Gautier writes of a character with a "petit œil vert de mer," and later uses "l'œil glauque." It becomes, in fact, such a characteristic word in the poetic vocabulary of the century that Pound used it as typical of the Nineties in France and wrote in "A Study of French Poets," in the course of discussing Stuart Merrill:

The period was "glauque" and "nacre," it had its pet and too-petted adjectives, the handles of parody; but it had also a fine care for sound, for sound fine-wrought, not mere swish and resonant rumble, not

> "Dolores, O hobble and kobble Dolores.
> O perfect obstruction on track."

The particular sort of fine workmanship shown in this sonnet of Merrill's has of late been too much let go by the board. One may do worse than compare it with the Syrian syncopation of $\Delta\iota\acute{\omega}\nu\alpha$ and $"A\delta\omega\nu\iota\nu$ in Bion's Adonis.

The phrase, then, has its overtones of parody for Pound, showing that despite his allegiance to Swinburne and Rossetti as against Gladstone and Ruskin he is aware of the two poets' limitations. To return to *Yeux Glauques*, one can set beside a number of Pound's descriptive phrases—"Thin like brook-water, with a vacant gaze," "The thin clear gaze," "questing and passive"— a similar series from *Cærulei Oculi*—"les langueurs de leurs prunelles," "leur transparence verdâtre," "son reflet clair," "l'abîme de ce regard," "ce regard céruléen"—that have entered into their shaping.

A relation somewhat like that between *Yeux Glauques* aud *Cærulei Oculi* exists between the tenth poem of *Mauberley*'s first section and *Fumée* in *Émaux et Camées*, with the stylist's leaking thatched roof and the creaking door derived in part from

> Là-bas, sous les arbres s'abrite
> Une chaumière au dos bossu;
> Le toit penche, le mur s'effrite,
> Le seuil de la porte est moussu.

And much of the spirit of Pound's condemnation of the stylist's economic exile from society is found in *La Mansarde*, in which Gautier, refusing to "lie like an author," insists

> Pour la grisette et pour l'artiste,
> Pour le veuf et pour le garçon,
> Une mansarde est toujours triste:
> Le grenier n'est beau qu'en chanson.

One could go on at length pairing words and phrases from *Mauberley* and *Émaux et Camées*. "Venus Anadyomène," "profil," "carton," "mousseline," "chefs-d'œuvre morts-nés," to mention a few, find their echoes in *Mauberley*. Some of the words and phrases are part of the vocabulary of nineteenth-century French verse. Laforgue, for example, is probably as much responsible as Gautier for Pound's use of "still-born" and "mousseline." But most of them came to Pound direct from

Émaux et Camées, and it is clear that before he became the instigator Pound was always the assimilator.

Yet there is more of Gautier in *Mauberley* than this kind of adaptation. The two key poems in the first section, the section dominated by Pound himself, are II ("The age demanded an image") and III ("The tea-rose tea-gown, etc.") in which Pound renders judgment on postwar London, contrasting its demands and emphases with those of a classic golden age. The two poems give to the entire first section its dominant tone, and without them the remainder of the suite is unintelligible. They are also the two poems that derive most completely from *Émaux et Camées* and the general body of Gautier's work.

Here the material from Gautier enters into vocabulary, general tone, and basic theme, starting with emphasis on the Attic virtues and becoming more pronounced with "not, not assuredly alabaster" and "the 'sculpture' of rhyme" with its echo of "sculpte, lime, cisèle" from *L'Art*. "The tea-rose tea-gown, etc." continues the influence, revealing now the double use to which Pound puts *Émaux et Camées* as he derives both the classic theme and its contemporary degradation from Gautier. *Émaux et Camées* contains an entire poem, *La Rose-Thé*, to the tea-rose, and, more importantly related here, another poem which mentions the tea-rose and also combines the pagan and modern themes in its opening stanzas. It is *À Une Robe Rose*, which begins:

> Que tu me plais dans cette robe
> Qui te déshabille si bien,
> Faisant jaillir ta gorge en globe,
> Montrant tout nu ton bras païen!
>
> Frêle comme une aile d'abeille,
> Frais comme un cœur de rose-thé,
> Son tissu, caresse vermeille,
> Voltige autour de ta beauté.

The poem closes with the sort of artificial sentiment that annoys Pound:

> Et ces plis roses sont les lèvres
> De mes désirs inapaisés,
> Mettant au corps dont tu les sèvres
> Une tunique de baisers.

The second stanza of Pound's poem announces the central theme of his denunciation with

> Christ follows Dionysus,
> Phallic and ambrosial
> Made way for macerations;

and it is here that one is struck not only with the parallel to the theme of *Bûchers et Tombeaux* from *Émaux et Camées*, specifically

> Des dieux que l'art toujours révère
> Trônaient au ciel marmoréen;
> Mais l'Olympe cède au Calvaire,
> Jupiter au Nazaréen;

but is led directly into the preface of *Mademoiselle de Maupin*, that first detailed exposition of Art-for-Art's-sake which, to the English reader, seems to come too soon in the nineteenth century. Early in it Gautier declares: "Mais c'est la mode maintenant d'être vertueux et chrétien, c'est une tournure qu'on se donne; on se pose en saint Jerome comme autrefois en don Juan; l'on est pâle et maceré. . . ." It appears quite characteristic of Pound's method that from these centers in Gautier he extracts the theme of latter-day maceration without carrying over Gautier's tone of witty exaggeration.

There are other indications that *Mademoiselle de Maupin* may have been an influence in the composition of *Hugh Selwyn Mauberley*. The whole of the ninth chapter is a discussion of Christianity and the modern world and deals with the celebration of beauty. "J'aime mieux la Venus Anadyomène, mille fois mieux," says the narrator, and later enters into a discussion of his his own imitations of classic love poetry, a discussion which, though it never names Propertius, calls him instantly to mind with repeated references to Cynthia.

Whether or not Pound drew directly from *Mademoiselle de Maupin*—and the "maceration" would lead one to think that at least the preface was fresh in his mind—is not as important as the close parallel between the entire first section of *Mauberley* and the tone of Gautier's reaction to his own world as expressed in *Émaux et Camées*. Taking the second and third poems of *Mauberley* as the strongest echo of this reaction, one can see how it reaches out and colors almost every poem in the first section. One sees it in the neglected M. Verog, parallel to the neglected Napoleonic veterans of *Vieux de la Vieille*—"Ils furent le jour dont nous sommes / Le soir et peut-être la nuit"; in Mr. Nixon's column—"Mes colonnes sont alignées / Au portique du feuilleton; / Elles supportent résignées / Du journal le pesant fronton." (*Après le Feuilleton*); in the tone of the drawing-room scene— "Les dandys et les diplomates, / Sur leurs faces à teintes mates, / Ne montrant rien." (*La Bonne Soirée*); and even in the color of the *Envoi*'s roses, "red overwrought with orange"—"De chaudes teintes orangées / Dorent sa joue au fard vermeil;" (*Le Château du Souvenir*). And perhaps more profoundly influential than all these, the parallel between the *Préface* of *Émaux et Camées*, with its reference to Goethe in Weimar ignoring "les guerres de l'empire" and writing "*le Divan occidental*," suggesting to Gautier that he too ignore "l'ouragan / Qui fouettait mes vitres fermées," leading to *Mauberley*'s stylist in retreat from "the world's welter."

So strongly did Gautier come to stand for Pound as one who reacted against the pressures of his time that Pound returned to him a few years later in this exact connection. In his "Paris Letter" dated August, 1922, published in the September issue of *The Dial*, Pound discussed René Descharmes' recent study *Autour de Bouvard et Pécuchet*. Writing on Flaubert's relation to the nineteenth century, Pound turned also to Gautier, quoting from both *Après le Feuilleton* and *Bûchers et Tombeaux*, neither quotation appearing in Descharmes' work:

Gautier, poor all his life, driven from one bit of hack work to another (*Mes colonnes sont alignées*) reacts in his Olympian perfection:

> "Le squelette était invisible
> Au temps heureux de l'Art païen;
> L'homme, sous la forme sensible,
> Content du beau, ne cherchait rien."

and Flaubert who until his quixotic abandonment of his fortune had been "able to keep out of it," Flaubert capable of his great engineering feat, reacts in his huge labour of drainage and sanitation, beginning as Descharmes so intelligently points out, "When as a small child, he was already registering the imbecile remarks of an old lady who had come on a visit to his father."

Moving on to the twentieth century as inheritor of the nineteenth, Pound then concluded with a denunciation of the "average mind" written in the same spirit as the denunciation in *Mauberley*:

And this average mind is our king, our tyrant, replacing Oedipus and Agamemnon in our tragedy.

It is this human stupidity that elects the Wilsons and LL. Georges and puts power into the hands of the gun-makers, demanding that they blot out the sunlight, that they crush out the individual and the perception of beauty. This flabby blunt-wittedness is the tyrant.

Pound's close association of Gautier and Flaubert goes far to explain the absence of any very apparent traces of "his true Penelope," whose work he was using at the time in *Canto VII*. Pound may have drawn at least one suggestion quite unconsciously from Flaubert; for though I feel certain that the second stanza of *Cærulei Oculi* and the title of the poem itself were the immediate sources of the phrase "yeux glauques," possibly reinforced by the passages already quoted from *Mademoiselle de Maupin*,

Flaubert uses the words in *L'Éducation Sentimentale* to describe the eyes of M. Dambreuse: "Une énergie impitoyable reposait dans ses yeux glauques, plus froids que des yeux de verre."

In spite of Gautier's almost complete displacement of Flaubert for *Mauberley*, Flaubert is still demonstrably present, though in a series of passages where one would least expect to find him: Hugh Selwyn Mauberley's voyage of revery among the Pacific islands. All but two of the physical details used in description of the Moluccas here are little more than the standard clichés of the archipelago. But two details are altogether out of the ordinary—the flamingoes and the simoon. They are out of the ordinary because they are altogether out of place geographically, there being no flamingoes in the Moluccas and the sand-laden wind of Africa and Persia carrying no farther than India. What we have here is Carthage and Flaubert's African travels, with the birds' very natural pose possibly suggested by "l'ibis rose" and "l'ibis, le bec dans son jabot" of Gautier's *Nostalgies d'Obélisques*. The palms, the coral, the sand, the quiet water, the flamingoes, all occur early in *Salammbô*, with a specific passage in the third chapter intimately related to *Mauberley*:

Autour de Carthage les ondes immobiles resplendissaient, car la lune étalait sa lueur tout à la fois sur le golfe environné de montagnes et sur le lac de Tunis, où des phénicoptères parmi les bancs de sable formaient de longues lignes roses, tandis, qu'au delà, sous les catacombes, la grande lagune salée miroitait comme un morceau d'argent. La voûte du ciel bleu s'enfonçait à l'horizon, d'un côté dans le poudroiement des plaines, de l'autre dans les brumes de la mer....

An indication of the closeness of Gautier and Flaubert similar to the "yeux glauques" of *L'Éducation Sentimentale* occurs in Flaubert's description of Schahabarim, high priest of the goddess Tanit, as "ce pâle eunuqe exténué de macérations." *Salammbô* may, however, have contributed quite basically to Pound's thinking at this time, or at least reinforced the trend of his economic analysis. Flaubert's painstaking investigation of the Carthaginian economy is reflected in a number of scattered passages, one of which is of particular interest in relation to Pound's own theories, not so much for its mention of Jewish usury as for its inclusion of public and private debts:

> D'abord, le pouvoir dépendait de tous sans qu'aucun fût assez fort pour l'accaparer. Les dettes particulières étaient considérées comme dettes publiques, les hommes de race chananéenne avaient le monopole du commerce; en multipliant les bénéfices de la piraterie par ceux de l'usure, en exploitant, rudement les terres, les esclaves et les pauvres, quelquefois on arrivait à la richesse.

Despite this detour into Flaubert, the pervasiveness of Gautier on all levels is impressive evidence of the influence of *Émaux et Camées* upon *Mauberley*. It is indicative, too, of Pound's rapid assimilation of his reading and re-reading, and, his translator's techniques fully mastered, of his ability to seize instantly the color and tone of his materials. That other influences are also present in *Mauberley* is clear; for the echoes of Gautier disappear almost completely after the turning away from the "eau-forte par Jacquemart," until they reappear, muted, in the *Medallion*, itself a reminder of Gautier's "médaille austère" with its references to Venus and amber.

Whether or not Pound turned back to Gautier's *Poésies Complètes* in addition to *Émaux et Camées*, as Eliot had done when he drew on *L'Hippopotame* for *The Hippopotamus*, is impossible to say with certainty. If he did, he may have been moved with some force by the apparently impromptu poem Gautier wrote on the back of a letter in 1846, in which, as a prospective colonist, he applied to the Minister of War for an Algerian land-grant. The lines read:

> Sur la montaigne de la vie,
> Au plateau de trente-cinq ans,
> Soufflent mes coursiers, haletants,
> De la chimère poursuivie.

> Je reste là quelques instants
> Brisé, mais l'âme inassouvie,
> Promenant mon regard glacé
> Sur l'avenir et le passé.

For in 1919 Pound himself was in his thirty-fifth year, and *Mauberley* stands in some measure as a pause on the plateau as Pound is forced to a personal decision and determines to leave London. Whether or not he looked at these lines during his review of Gautier's "rhyme and strophe," it is at least safe to say that *Hugh Selwyn Mauberley* would not be quite the poem it is had it been modeled on the *Bay Psalm Book*, assuming a copy of the latter ready to hand.

3 syrian syncopation

Mauberley's metrics, however, are not drawn from *Émaux et Camées* alone. Pound's remarks already quoted on the "glauque" character of the nineteenth century and the strength of Merrill's sonnet contain the needed clue here, though without further direction from Pound it would almost certainly go unnoticed. When René Taupin wrote "C'est ce que Pound a fait dans *Mauberley* en combinant Byron et Gautier—" he may have been recording a personal conviction or reproducing a slightly inaccurate international exchange. There are some obvious temptations in Byron: the denunciation of English society, the farewell to England, the personal display. And there is some Byron in *Émaux et Camées*—"le Manfred du ruisseau," "le Kaled d'un Lara"—but it scarcely seems a part of what attracted Pound to Gautier. Pound's *Letters* includes one communication with Taupin, dated from Vienna in 1927, in which Pound emphasizes the importance of Gautier in his own poetry and asks: "Est-ce-que on peut causer?—ici maintenant ou à Rapallo en Juillet'" I do not know if this meeting ever occurred, but if it did and the conversation turned to *Mauberley* Pound would probably have said something similar to what he wrote Felix Schelling in 1922: "The metre in *Mauberley* is Gautier and

Bion's 'Adonis'; or at least those are the two grafts I was trying to flavour it with. Syncopation from the Greek; and a general distaste for the slushiness and swishiness of the post-Swinburnian British line." Byron or no, Bion is certainly here.

Pound could have found no better model than Bion for a metrical pattern to play off against Gautier's exact stanzas. Rather than attempt an independent analysis for which I am not fitted, I paraphrase some of Professor Philippe Legrand's comments on Bion's verse from the second volume of his *Bucoliques Grecs*: "The form, as well as the spirit, distinguishes the *Epitaph* from the epic compositions in the antique mode. There is no question here of hunting for 'strophes'; the fragments that follow upon each other, which the repeated cries of grief enclose and set off like a refrain, are of quite unequal length. . . . Repetitions of many kinds are frequent: repetition of a phrase which is brought back like an echo; repetition of the same word in two (in certain instances, symmetrical) parallel phrases; repetition of a word within the same phrase. . . . Here and there . . . these repetitions, seeming to translate a hesitation, an effort towards greater exactness, greater sincerity, give to the expression something singularly touching. Combined with the balance of phrases different in form but similar in content, they produce in the end an effect of exhaustion, of morbid languishing, like assiduously repeated incantations."

It is the play of these broken rhythms, these fragments, against the severe quatrains of *Émaux et Camées* that produces *Mauberley*'s metrical patterns in all their variety. The syncopation begins early, in the first poem as an examination of the semicolon s use will show, but it is never a fixed thing, for it builds up in the second poem to the insistent repetitions of "Not, at any rate, an Attic grace; / Not, not certainly, the obscure reveries," and the later echo of "not, not assuredly, alabaster." The stricter form dominates in the third poem, though Pound still uses a complex vowel pattern here and the strongly emphasized pause, as in "Defects—after Samothrace"; but in the fourth

poem the Greek model takes over almost entire. Anyone inter-
ested in Pound's brilliant adaptation of rhythmic patterns, his
ability to reproduce entire systems of sound, should set beside

> Some quick to arm,
> some for adventure,
> some for fear of weakness,
> some for fear of censure,
> some for love of slaughter, in imagination,
> learning later . . .
> some in fear, learning love of slaughter;

these lines from Bion, in which the Loves pay tribute to the dead
Adonis:

> Χὼ μὲν ὀϊστώς,
> ὃς δ'ἐπὶ τόξον ἔβαλλ',
> ὃς δὲ πτερόν,
> ὃς δὲ φαρέτραν.
> Χὼ μὲν ἔλυσε πέδιλον Ἀδώνιδος
> οἱ δὲ λέβητι
> χρυσείῳ φορέοισιν ὕδωρ,
> ὁ δε μηρία λούει,
> ὃς δ'ὄπιθεν πτερύγεσσιν ἀναψύχει τὸν Ἄδωνιν. [7]

Here Pound, seizing upon Bion's most characteristic devices,
heightens and extends the repetition and reinforces it with
rhyme.

Another example of Bion's influence in the poem occurs in
the second poem of the "Mauberley" section, where Pound,
taking up Bion's device of the hesitating rhythm, stresses it

---

[7] For the sake of the rhythm it may be useful to transliterate here.
Cho men oistos, / os d'epi toxon eball, os de pteron, os de pharetran. /
Cho men elyse pedilon Adonidos, oi de lebeti / chryseio phoreoisin udor,
o de meria loyei, / os d'opithen pterygessin anapsychei ton Adonin.
"One puts his arrows on the funeral bed, one his bow, one a feather
from his wing, one his quiver. This one unties Adonis' sandal, others
carry water in a golden bowl; one washes the wounds, one, standing
behind Adonis, fans him with his wings." (Ll. 81–85.)

through his punctuation and repetitions to produce "Drifted . . . drifted precipitate," and "To be certain . . . certain . . ." In other passages, the "syncopation" is not always so immediately apparent. Perhaps its most quiet modulation occurs in the "Conservatrix of Milésien" stanzas, particularly in the play upon the "er" syllables, in which "bank-clerkly" poses another international problem; whereas the closest echo of the sound pattern derived from the two classical names is the line "Luini in porcelain."

As for the metrics derived from Gautier, possibly the most revealing insight into their use can be obtained through an examination of Pound's adaptations of the strictest stanza in *Émaux et Camées* and the way in which he introduces variations upon it until it is finally reproduced almost (though never quite) exactly near the end of the suite. This is the chiseled, cameolike quatrain of *L'Art*:

> Oui, l'œuvre sort plus belle
> D'une forme au travail
> Rebelle,
> Vers, marbre, onyx, émail.

Much adapted, it makes its first appearance in *Mauberley* in *Yeux Glauques* as

> Thin like brook-water,
> With a vacant gaze.
> The English Rubaiyat was still-born
> In those days.

and

> Bewildered that a world
> Shows no surprise
> At her last maquero's
> Adulteries.

It reappears in the twelfth poem as the basis for such a stanza as

> Poetry, her border of ideas,
> The edge, uncertain, but a means of blending
> With other strata
> Where the lower and higher have ending;

but does not announce itself completely until the "Mauberley" section, where it is clearly revealed, but not slavishly reproduced, throughout the first poem, and never more distinctly than when both the form and the theme of *L'Art* are joined:

> Firmness,
> Not the full smile,
> His art, but an art
> In profile;

a stanza that combines Gautier at his strictest with Bion's repetition.

The stanza from *L'Art* is perhaps a little less obvious as the base for the lines already quoted in part to illustrate the use of Bion's hesitation, lines that again reveal Pound as the complete technician:

> To be certain ... certain ...
> (Amid aerial flowers) ... time for arrangements—
> Drifted on
> To the final estrangement;

but Pound's variations are not completed until the fourth poem of the "Mauberley" section, the poem that concludes Mauberley's history. Here the technical interest derives from the cut line, which for two stanzas is made up of three syllables—"Tawn fore-shores," "Flamingoes"—and is then shortened to two syllables, as in *L'Art*, the cut line placed differently each time it is used:

> A consciousness disjunct,
> Being but this overblotted
> Series
> Of intermittences;

Coracle of Pacific voyages,
The unforecasted beach;
Then on an oar
Read this:

"I was
"And I no more exist;
"Here drifted
"An hedonist."

Mauberley is a poem of great metrical subtlety, but the subtlety yields readily to anyone who has Pound's methods and sources as keys.

There is a trace more of Bion to be examined, however. Bion's themes are not reproduced—unless one wishes to insist that both poems are elegiac—but a few phrases common to the Bucolics do appear. They are all commonplaces, nevertheless, and there is little to be made of τὸ καλὸν and τὸ αγαθὸν as far as the *Epitaph* is concerned. The most interesting connection with Bion is the opening of the "Mauberley" section's second poem:

For three years, diabolus in the scale,
He drank ambrosia,
All passes, ANANGKE prevails
Came end, at last, to that Arcadia.

He had moved amid her phantasmagoria,
Amid her galaxies,
NUKTIS 'AGALMA

The use of "Anangke" here suggests an echo of the "figured poem" *The Wings*, usually included in anthologies of the Bucolics, with Eros' mention of his birth under the reign of Necessity. But the real problem is "NUKTIS 'AGALMA"— "Night's ornament"—which has ridden through all texts of *Mauberley* despite its combination of Greek root and Latin genitive, as if this "variant," once established, had been stubbornly stuck to by its creator. The phrase, however, is not original with Pound. Anyone who has followed Pound's reading learns to go well beyond the immediate reference given. Reading beyond the *Epitaph*, one finds, in what Legrand gives as the eighth fragment:

"Ἕσπερε, τᾶς ἐρατᾶς χρύσεον φάος Ἀφρογενείας,
"Ἕσπερε, κυανέας ἱερὸν, φίλε, Νυκτὸς ἄγαλμα.[8]

The source here is of some importance, for it makes unnecessary any speculation on the possibility of reading ἄγαλμα as "beautiful statue"—though Pound may well intend this as a secondary meaning—while the reference to Hesperus, the evening star (Venus), when read in relation with "her galaxies," reinforces, as I shall show later, the entire Venus-pattern of the poem. And the identification of this phrase is, finally, another indication of Pound's inability to adapt a form, to use a model, without taking over with it something in color, in theme, in quotation.

---

[8] Hesperus, golden light of loving Aphrodite ("the foam-born"), dear Hesperus, shadowy blue Night's ornament.

4 the major james

In the same letter to Felix Schelling in which Pound spoke of
the two grafts from Gautier and Bion, he also wrote:

(Of course I'm no more Mauberley than Eliot is Prufrock. Mais
passons.) Mauberley is a mere surface. Again a study in form, an attempt
to condense the James novel. Meliora speramus.

Leaving for the moment the question of *Mauberley*'s being a
mere surface, and the more important question of how casual a
poet's choice of masks can be, an inspection of *Mauberley* as
Pound's condensation of the James novel offers a number of in-
sights into the poem.

When the editors of *Hound and Horn* asked Pound for a con-
tribution to their April : June, 1934 number—the Henry James
issue that played so large a part in the James "revival"—they
received in reply a post card that read:

Melbourne, Monday (15 Jan.)—Rudyard Kipling has agreed to write
an ode for the dedication of the city's Shrine of Remembrance. Paris
edtn. N. Y. Herald 16 Jan.

Pound no doubt felt privileged to answer in this manner because
he had undertaken, more than fifteen years earlier, a complete

survey of Henry James's work for the *Little Review* (August and September, 1918). The study had been reprinted in *Instigations* (1920) and the Yale Press was preparing to include it in *Make It New*, to be published in 1935.

This survey, which Pound called his "Baedeker to a continent," is filled with revealing comments on both James and Pound himself; for Pound clearly felt a personal relationship with his older fellow-expatriate. Late in the essay he remarks that "only an American who has come abroad will ever draw *all* the succulence from Henry James's writings; one has perhaps a purely personal, selfish, unliterary sense of intimacy; with, in my own case, the vast unbridgeable difference of settling-in and escape. The essence of James is that he is always 'settling-in,' it is the ground-tone of his genius."

But beyond this sense of relationship the most important part of his study for an understanding of *Mauberley* is Pound's statement of what he considered his own private perception of James as a fighter against pressures:

I am tired of hearing pettiness talked about Henry James's style. The subject has been discussed enough in all conscience, along with the minor James. Yet I have heard no word of the major James, of the hater of tyranny; book after early book against oppression, the domination of modern life; not worked out in the diagrams of Greek tragedy, not labeled "epos" or "Æschylus." The outbursts in *The Tragic Muse*, the whole of *The Turn of the Screw*, human liberty, personal liberty, the rights of the individual against all sorts of intangible bondage.* The passion of it, the continual passion of it in this man who, fools said, didn't "feel." I have never yet found a man of emotion against whom idiots didn't raise this cry.

Certainly one of *Mauberley*'s major themes is the pressure of society exerted upon the individual, the "demands of the age"

---

* This holds, despite anything that may be said. . . . What he fights is "influence," the impinging of family pressure, the impinging of one personality on another etc. etc. [Note in *Instigations*.]

that Hugh Selwyn Mauberley cannot satisfy and that lead in the end to his isolation and death.

As Hugh Kenner has pointed out, *Mauberley*'s most literal connection with the James novel is the passage that reads

> He had moved amid her phantasmagoria,
> Amid her galaxies,

a strong echo of Lambert Strether's remark to Maria Gostrey near the end of *The Ambassadors*, when he declares:

"Of course I moved among miracles. It was all phantasmagoric. . . ."

Yet if we are to take Strether as the Jamesian hero and the person of Mauberley as Pound's rehandling of this figure, a number of differences must be noted. At the close of *The Ambassadors* Strether is presented with a choice. Maria Gostrey in effect offers herself to him—offers herself, Paris, Europe, the world that he has discovered so late in his life. And Strether's rejection of this offer, his withdrawal, his entire renunciation of the European possibilities is founded upon what is at least overtly a moral base, a refusal at this point *not* to return to Mrs. Newsome, *not* to carry out, possibly simply as a duty now, a plan that had once seemed to him in the nature of a reward. Mauberley, on the other hand, has no such choice to make. In one of the most apparently obscure sections of *Mauberley*, after the minor poet's emergence in the poem, Mauberley is revealed as incapable of enjoying his "great affect." This is the poem that opens with an epigraph by "Caid Ali"—who is Ezra Pound himself, on his own testimony to Kimon Friar—and the poem moves throughout on two levels: one the level of orchid as aerial flower and iris as earthly flower, the other the level of orchid as ὄρχις (testicle) and the diastasis of the eyes as invitation to active love. Mauberley, recognizing too late the opportunities offered him, and finding himself now utterly set apart from anything but the world that he explores within himself, is left by "mandate of Eros" only the frozen stone dog of memory snapping without motion after unattainable passion. If it seems gratuitous to insist

on the erotic content of "Eros," one can at least quote from
Cabaret Dancers:

> Or take the intaglio, my fat great-uncle's heirloom:
> Cupid, astride a phallus with two wings,
> Swinging a cat-o'-nine-tails.

Critical writing on Henry James has proliferated so since
1918 that it would be foolish to discuss in detail here Pound's
version of the James novel from the point of view of its general
validity; but it is at least worth suggesting that by this condensa-
tion, this simplification of motive, Pound has stripped back a few
covering layers and has stated more openly than the original what
lurks in the deeper levels of James's text. Though Lambert
Strether's rejection is never stated in specifically sexual terms,
many of his remarks to Chad Newsome and Mme de Vionnet
and Maria Gostrey do show that beneath the surface of his mind
some suspicion of incapacity exists.[9] And it is at this point in
Pound's poem that one senses not only the Jamesian hero but
also the figure of Henry James himself in all his own personal
and sexual ambiguity hovering behind the mask of Hugh Selwyn
Mauberley. Remembering this, one realizes that the reference to
Abelard in *I Vecchii*, the seventh poem of *Moeurs Contemporaines*,
as Pound reports a conversation with Henry James is probably
no accident:

> Il était comme un tout petit garçon
> With his blouse full of apples

---

[9] That this was a thoroughly conscious part of James's intention is
shown by his notebook entry dated *October 19th*, 1901, *Lamb House*.
"Something in reference to man who, like W.[illiam] D.[ean]
H.[owells] (say), has never known *at all* any woman BUT his wife—
and at 'time of life' somehow sees it, is face to face with it: little situation
on it. *Ça rentre*, however, rather, into the idea (is a small side of it) of
The Ambassadors. But *never*, NEVER—in any degree to call a relation
at all: *and on American lines.* xxxxx" (*The Notebooks of Henry James*,
p. 313.)

And sticking out all the way round;
Blagueur! "Con gli occhi onesti e tardi,"

And he said:
"Oh! Abelard!" as if the topic
Were much too abstruse for his comprehension,
And he talked about "the Great Mary,"
And said: "Mr. Pound is shocked at my levity,"
When it turned out he meant Mrs. Ward.

Not only does the person of Mauberley enjoy a relationship with the Jamesian hero, the entire suite of *Mauberley* enjoys a structural relation with the novels of James as seen by Pound. An awareness of this saves one from the error of identifying Pound and Mauberley and emphasizes Mauberley's deliberately late emergence as an independent figure. In using this delayed presentation of the central figure, Pound almost parodies a Jamesian characteristic that he remarks on in his study:

He appears at times to write around and around a thing and not always to emerge from the "amorous plan" of what he wanted to present, into definite presentation.

One can read all of *Mauberley*, then, as an elaborate metrical exercise in the form of a condensed James novel; for nowhere in his writing on James does Pound indicate that James actually varied his method, tending in his later work to come more immediately to grips with his themes and characters.

Another parallel between James and *Mauberley* probably occurs in the poem entitled "*The Age Demanded*." Here Mauberley, cut off from the world, drifts into his revery, and as he drifts the words of the poem become increasingly abstract and general, the movement of the verse repetitive and twice interrupted by visions of "the coral isle" and "the unexpected palms." Here we have, I suspect, a derivation from the Jamesian conversational style, a fascination to everyone subjected to it. Pound opens his essay by describing it:

The massive head, the slow uplift of the hand, *gli occhi onesti e tardi*, the long sentences piling themselves up in elaborate phrase after phrase, the lightning incision, the pauses, the slight shaking admonitory gesture with its "wu-a-wait a little, wait a little, something will come;" blague and benignity and the weight of so many years' careful, incessant labor of minute observation always there to enrich the talk.

Indeed, Pound was so fascinated by the manner and his own description of it that he used it again in *Canto VII*:

> And the great domed head, *con gli occhi onesti e tardi*
> Moves before me, phantom with weighted motion,
> *Grave incessu*, drinking the tone of things,
> And the old voice lifts itself
> > weaving an endless sentence.

To pause for an examination of the Italian phrase Pound almost invariably uses when he writes of James may seem an intolerably imitative interruption at this point, but the phrase has its importance for *Mauberley*. Pound created it by combining two similar passages from *The Divine Comedy*: *con occhi tardi e gravi* (*Inf.* IV, 112) and *E nel mover de gli occhi onesta e tarda* (*Purg.* VI, 63). The significant reference is the second one, not so much because it is the literal base of Pound's phrase but because Dante is here describing Sordello. Not only is this a natural center for Pound, with his interest in the troubadours, to use (and as one who has written of Browning: "Und überhaupt ich stamm aus Browning. Pourquoi nier son père?") but its focus upon Sordello reminds one that Dante presents him in the role of critic of his times and contemporaries, one who stood out against the pressures of tyrants and the debased values of his age. Thus, once again, and from so great a distance, the Jamesian extensions round back into the themes of *Mauberley*.

Most of the echoes in *Mauberley* from Pound's immediate sources are so directly apparent, so consciously presented as quotation, translation, or paraphrase, that one may hesitate to suggest that he also caught up certain tones, certain phrases, quite unconsciously. Much of the Gautier vocabulary is surely used deliberately, just as the restatement of Strether's remark is a deliberate introduction of the Jamesian theme. Yet, considering this direct indebtedness to *The Ambassadors*, it is interesting to note that all Pound had to say of the novel in his grand survey was

1903. "The Ambassadors," rather clearer than the other work. Etude of Paris vs. Woollett. Exhortation to the idle, well-to-do, to leave home.

In view of this scant tribute it is worth suggesting, as illustrative of the absorptive qualities of Pound's mind, that he probably picked up a series of hints and phrases from another volume that he mentioned even more casually:

Perhaps one covers the ground by saying that the James of this period is "light literature," entertaining if one have nothing better to do. Neither "Terminations" nor (1896) "Embarrassments" would have founded a reputation.

The interesting title here is *Embarrassments*. Though Pound used the New York edition for quotations in his study, his "Baedeker" reviews the works in the order of their original publication and as individual books. Since *Embarrassments* does not appear as a unit in the New York edition, which reprints only two of its four longish stories, Pound would have been looking at either the Macmillan or the Heinemann volume, each dated 1896.

Embarrassments is made up of *The Figure in the Carpet*, *Glasses*, *The Next Time*, and *The Way It Came*. In the first, and best known, of these stories, the narrator is a young literary man in London to whom the great novelist Hugh Vereker reveals that there is a great uniting theme, a string that his "pearls are strung on," running through all his books. The narrator learns this because he has written a review of Vereker's latest work for *The Middle*, a weekly journal to which both he and his friend George Corvick contribute. "I had written on Hugh Vereker, but never a word in *The Middle*, where my dealings were mainly with the ladies and the minor poets," remarks the narrator, and he goes on to explain that he had accepted an invitation to the country house of Lady Jane, a literary hostess, only because she had assured him that Vereker would be there. After a long pursuit of Hugh Vereker's "figure in the carpet," the narrator finds himself baffled and confides in Corvick, who, in the company of Gwendolen Erme, the girl he hopes to marry, immediately takes up the search. The engagement of Gwendolen and Corvick founders for lack of funds, and Mrs. Erme's approval, but Corvick does at last find "the figure" while he is on a journalistic assignment in India. In the course of his return he stops off in Italy to verify his findings with Vereker, and, writing to Gwendolen, who now assures the narrator that she and Corvick are and have always been engaged, he remarks on the wonder of his discovery. In a passage based on this letter, James delivers his own judgment of "the age":

When once it came out it came out, was there with a splendour that made you ashamed; and there had not been, save in the bottomless vulgarity of the age, with every one tasteless and tainted, every sense stopped, the smallest reason why it should have been overlooked.

The narrator is prevented by what he refers to once as "the march of occurrences" and a little later as "the procession of events," from seeing Corvick on his return. A few days after the marriage, Corvick is killed in a carriage accident, and the narrator is never able to learn the secret from Corvick's widow or, after her death, from her second husband, who, indeed, never even knew that such a secret lay in his wife's possession.

Glasses is told by a portrait painter. Its central figure is Flora Louisa Saunt, a girl of slender means whose face is her great asset and pride. She conceals as long as she can that her sight is threatened, in the hope of marrying Lord Iffield, heir to Lord Considine, refusing to wear the gogglelike glasses with a bar across them that might save her sight. The artist-narrator describes his first impression of her, noting that the "head, the features, the colour, the whole facial oval and radiance had a

wonderful purity." And later, commenting on the possibility of
Flora's wearing glasses, he speaks of trying "to fix this sudden
image of Flora's face glazed in and cross-barred. . . ." The artist
decides to "have a go at her head," and an awkward young man,
Geoffrey Dawling, falls in love with the portrait. "He was the
young prince in the legend or the comedy who loses his heart to
the miniature of an outland princess." Flora loses Iffield when
she is pushed to a confession of the danger her sight is in, but
some years later the artist, returning from America, sees her in
her box at a performance of *Lohengrin*, radiantly beautiful. She
appears to recognize him; he enters her box, to discover that she
is blind, that she has accepted Dawling, and that she lives utterly
content in the knowledge that she is more beautiful than ever.
As the opera resumes, the three of them sit listening. "If the
music, in that darkness, happily soared and swelled for her, it beat
its wings in unison with those of a gratified passion. A great deal
came and went between us without profaning the occasion. . . ."

The Next Time is the story of Ray Limbert, who is too fine a
writer to succeed with the novel-reading public, and is recounted
by a friend who is another of James's young literary men about
London. After a try at writing for a paper Limbert is turned off
because "They want 'journalism.' They want tremendous
trash." His sister-in-law, Jane Highmore, a most successful
novelist, keeps giving him sound advice:

. . . I never heard her speak of the literary motive as if it were dis-
tinguishable from the pecuniary. She cocked up his hat, she pricked up
his prudence for him, reminding him that as one seemed to take one's
self so the silly world was ready to take one. It was a fatal mistake to be
too candid even with those who were all right—not to look and to talk
prosperous, not at least to pretend that one had beautiful sales. To listen
to her you would have thought the profession of letters a wonderful
game of bluff. Wherever one's idea began it ended somehow in inspired
paragraphs in the newspapers.

Driven at last to try writing for the public in order to marry,
Limbert produces what he thinks is a popular work, only to find

that he has done even better than before. As the narrator remarks to Mrs. Highmore: "It won't move one, as they say in Fleet Street. The book has extraordinary beauty." After his marriage, Limbert continues his attempts to write down to the public. Finally, with his wife and children, he moves to the country to "a damp old house at sixpence a year," where he at least escapes his mother-in-law, Mrs. Stannace, who is unwilling to put up with "mere tolerance in a cottage." Until he dies, Limbert continues to compose masterpieces under the impression at each try that he is at last hitting the novel-reading public's taste.

The Way It Came, later entitled *The Friends of the Friends*, is a ghost story, and a part of what Pound would scarcely call even "the minor James."

There is in all this something too much, perhaps, for coincidence, and yet not enough for deliberate imitation. The name Hugh mentioned in connection with minor poets, the literary hostess Lady Jane, the "bottomless vulgarity of the age," something close to *Mauberley*'s cliché "the march of events," the emphasis on eyes, the "facial oval" with its most ironic "glaze" ("The face-oval beneath the glaze, / Bright in its suave bounding-line"), the miniature, the mention of music and "not profaning the occasion" ("The grand piano / Utters a profane / Protest with her clear soprano."), the degradation of journalism and the trashiness of the press, the "successful" author's advice, Fleet Street, the stylist's withdrawal to the damp country cottage. Each is ordinary enough in itself, so ordinary that without the others it would not be worth noticing. Perhaps the most one can say is negative, that no other single volume of James's offers so many parallels and half-echoes.

If it were not for the conjunction of these scattered items, it would be foolish to mention what may be the oddest connection of all between *Embarrassments* and *Mauberley*. But with them, and remembering the use of the Jacquemart etching from *Émaux et Camées*, I am willing to hazard that Pound was looking at the Heinemann *Embarrassments*, which is bound in blue cloth and stamped on its front cover with a design of irises. Pound's use of the *Émaux et Camées* frontispiece is obviously deliberate; the use of *Embarrassments'* irises, if it is a use, is just as obviously unconscious, for *Mauberley's* "irides" deserve the merest side glance as flowers, and even as such, *Embarrassments*, as I shall show later, could not have been their primary source.

It is in the nature of this sort of evidence that it can never be conclusive of itself. What one needs is something outside *Mauberley*, and the normal place to look for it would be *Canto VII*, which contains the passage on James already quoted. There is a possible connection between this passage and *Embarrassments*, but it is so highly speculative a connection that it can hardly be used as final proof. The evidence lies in *grave incessu* (parallel to "with weighted motion"), which seems to be Pound's own phrase,[10] *grave* coming possibly from Dante's *tardi e gravi*. I suppose that anyone with a standard knowledge of Latin thinks automatically of only one line when he sees *incessu*: Virgil's *Vera incessu patuit dea. (Aen.* I, 405). When George Corvick cables to Gwendolen Erme that he has at last found the figure in the carpet, the narrator is skeptical and says to her: "But how does he know?" Gwendolen replies: "Know it's the real thing? Oh, I am sure when you see it you do know. *Vera incessu patuit dea.*"

What is most truly embarrassing in all this parallelism is its further richness when one remembers that George Corvick verifies his findings by calling on Hugh Vereker in Rapallo. Pound had visited Rapallo before 1920, but he did not establish himself there until 1924, after the Parisian interval. If there is anything to be made of this, it is more than I care to undertake here; but quite apart from this clairvoyant prefiguring, which would have enchanted the Henry James who wrote *The Way It Came* to the exact degree that it would irritate Ezra Pound, what

---

[10] I am not entirely certain of this, though one would expect from any classic source to find *gravi* in this construction.

I take to be the unconscious use of *Embarrassments*—or, for that matter, without taking it as a use at all but only as illustration of Jamesian phrasing, style, and theme; for the evidence can be played both ways—is another indication of the completeness with which Pound himself drank in "the tone of things."

An additional James-*Mauberley* connection—more exactly, a James-Gautier-*Mauberley* connection—remains to be examined. Much of the first part of Pound's study centers on James's *French Poets and Novelists*, which Pound calls "a point from which to measure Henry James's advance." It is the volume, also, that stands second in Pound's list of the essential James for the new reader, a list running to twenty titles, at the end of which Pound remarks: "If . . . the reader does not find delectation in the list given above, I think it fairly useless for him to embark on the rest." Pound uses *French Poets and Novelists* as a key to James's early critical views and attitudes. One feels the book's presence in remarks such as Pound's objection to James's "worst possible taste in pictures," which he describes as "almost as great a lack of taste as that which he attributes to the hackwork and newspaper critiques of Théophile Gautier," mentioning later that at the time (1876) James's taste in poetry was probably inclined to "the swish of De Musset." The book is so present in Pound's mind as a measure of James's critical development that the closing section of the James essay ("The Notes to 'The Ivory Tower' ") returns to it:

Retaining the name of the author, any faithful reader of James, or at any rate the attentive student, finds a good deal of amusement in deciphering the young James, his temperament as mellowed by recollection and here recorded forty years later, and then in contrasting it with the young James as revealed or even "betrayed" in his own early criticisms, "French Poets and Novelists," a much cruder and more savagely puritanical and plainly New England product with, however, certain permanent traits of his character already in evidence, and with a critical faculty keen enough to hit on certain weaknesses in the authors analyzed, often with profundity, and with often a "rightness" in his mistakes.

The Ivory Tower itself, emphasized also in the essay proper as an example of James's mastery of what commercialism meant to America, may have contributed something directly to *Mauberley*'s "tea-rose tea-gown etc." denunciation of the modern world from James's opening description of Rosanna Gaw, who, "mistress as she might have been of the most expensive modern aids to the constitution of a 'figure,' lived, as they said of her, in wrappers and tea-gowns . . ." Beyond this, however, and in the light of Pound's concentration upon and return to *French Poets and Novelists*, James's own essay on Gautier in that volume is worth looking at, particularly for the stress James places upon *Émaux et Camées* as the most characteristic of Gautier's poetry. The temptation to see in

> —Given that is his "fundamental passion,"
> This urge to convey the relation
> Of eye-lid and cheek-bone
> By verbal manifestations,

a rehandling of James's comment on Gautier's "intellectual passion" is strong, but as I have already noted, the 1920 state of the poem read simply

> Given, that is, his urge
> To convey the relation
> Of eye-lid and cheek-bone
> By verbal manifestation,

and the revision was probably made for other purposes. Nevertheless, the poem at the end of which James makes this comment is one of two poems by Gautier that he quotes in full, the only one from *Émaux et Camées*, and that particular poem is *L'Art*. Taking this with the other evidence, it is not particularly bold to think that James was one avenue leading Pound back to Gautier and to *Émaux et Camées* as metrical model.

5 physique de l'amour

If *Mauberley* is, as Pound has said, "a mere surface," it is a surface of considerable complexity, a surface, even, of some depth. But a surface must rest upon a foundation, and though it would be foolish to insist upon any single source other than Pound's own mind as ultimate base, it is still possible, I think, to push a little farther into the process of the poem's composition.

Hugh Kenner, certainly *Mauberley*'s most sensitive and sympathetic interpreter, asserts in a note in *The Poetry of Ezra Pound* that "the primary echo is as a matter of fact with Corbière," and writes in a later note:

At the time when *Mauberley* was written, Eliot was getting rid of Laforgue and in collaboration with Pound assimilating Corbière and Gautier. The Corbière reverberations are functional in Pound's poem, relating it to still more complex modes of self-knowledge than we have opportunity to go into here. At its deepest levels the poem is still virtually unread.

Pound himself, in the letter to René Taupin already quoted from, remarks (and in his own French): "Ce que vous prenez pour influence de Corbière est probablement influence direct de

Villon." To support this Villon-Corbière echo as *Mauberley*'s primary one, it would, I think, be necessary to insist that somewhere in the second section the ironic voice of the opening *Ode* speaks again, that Mauberley himself offers an obliquely personal commentary on Pound. But as I shall try to demonstrate shortly, the contrast here is so complete a one and of such a nature that it is ultimately a total dissociation. I believe that whatever there is of Villon or Corbière here is contained in the *Ode* and that what Kenner calls Pound's "impersonality" appears only in the "Mauberley" section, and even there, as I shall also try to show, merely on the surface. That the account of Mauberley himself "cannot be taken as an account of the poet of the *Cantos*" is certainly true, but only, I think, because the voice of the first section *is* the voice of the author of *The Cantos*. And though there is surely no need to accept at face value a poet's own statement of his sources and influences, Pound so automatically picks up and reproduces rhythm, theme, and vocabulary that it is difficult to believe without considerable evidence of this sort that the work of Corbière stands in more intimate relation to *Mauberley* than that of most of the poets discussed in "A Study in French Poets."

Another of these poets, however, Jules Laforgue, whose work Pound claimed, in writing to Taupin, he had used and understood even more thoroughly than Eliot had, has left important marks upon *Mauberley*. Warren Ramsey, in his excellent study *Jules Laforgue and the Ironic Inheritance*, notes how insistently Pound was concerned with Laforgue in various magazines at this time, expounding, translating, and paraphrasing, and points out the probability of Pound's deriving his use of dramatic contrast from Laforgue. Of *Mauberley* he writes:

One of Laforgue's favorite images, that of the foetus, turns up. The cliché, 'march of events,' is pressed into ironic service, according to characteristic Laforguian procedure. The verse depends on the literary reference as Laforgue's does, with 'l'an trentiesme de son eage' woven in. Here too are the long 'international' words out of Latin, the sort of polysyllables to which Laforgue resorted on slight pretext. At the end of the [fifth] quatrain, 'No adjunct to the Muses' diadem' furnishes a familiar ironic sparkle of grandeur. Taken singly, no one of these traits would justify the term 'Laforguian.' Occurring all together, sustained by the ironically learned tone which was Laforgue's contribution to nineteenth-century verse, they send us back to the Pierrot poems.

To this one might add that the shift from "sieve" to "seismograph" and the use of "the half-watt rays" in the "Mauberley" section probably derive from Laforgue's fascination with the "new" vocabulary of his century. They are exact illustrations of what Pound, writing on Laforgue in *Poetry* for November, 1917 ("Irony, Laforgue, and Some Satire"), calls his "verbalism," adding: "He has dipped his wings in the dye of scientific terminology."

At the same time, it may be instructive to look for a moment at Pound's use of "fœtus." When Eliot wrote

> In the palace of Mrs. Phlaccus, at Professor
> Channing-Cheetah's
> He laughed like an irresponsible fœtus,
> (*Mr. Apollinax*)

he was certainly using "one of Laforgue's favorite images." But when Pound wrote

> Among the pickled fœtuses and bottled bones,
> Engaged in perfecting the catalogue,
> I found the last scion of the
> Senatorial families of Strasbourg, Monsieur Verog,

he may have been pressing into service a word he was led to by Laforgue's repeated use of it, but he was using it primarily on an altogether literal level. Monsieur Verog is Pound's *nom de guerre* for Victor Gustave Plarr (1863–1929), friend of Lionel Johnson and Ernest Dowson, and author, among other works, of *In the Dorian Mood*. Plarr was Librarian of the Royal College of Surgeons when Pound knew him and he was indeed "among the pickled fœtuses and bottled bones," busy with the Library's catalogue, one half of which he completed in manuscript during his tenure of the office. If the word is Laforguian, its use is not, for it is precisely the use Gautier makes of it twice in descriptive passages of *Albertus*, first in the ninth stanza,

> Fœtus mal conservés saisissant d'une lieue
> L'odorat, et collant leur face jaune et bleue
> Contre le verre du bocal!

and again in the one hundred and twelfth stanza,

> Squelettes conservés dans les amphithéâtres,
> Animaux empaillés, monstres, fœtus verdâtres,
> Tout humides encor de leur bain d'alcool,
> Culs-de-jatte, pieds-bots, montés sur les limaces,
> Pendus tirant la langue et faisant des grimaces.

One should also point out that the first two lines of the stanza

> Conduct, on the other hand, the soul
> "Which the highest cultures have nourished"
> To Fleet St. where
> Dr. Johnson flourished,

are a translation of the first line of Laforgue's *Complainte des Pianos qu'on Entend dans les Quartiers Aisés*:

> Menez l'âme que les Lettres ont bien nourrie,
> Les pianos, les pianos, dans les quartiers aisés!

The lines reflect Pound's brilliance of tone as translator, rejecting the obvious "Letters" and hitting upon the freshly precise "highest cultures." They probably reflect even more than this, for the piano of the *Medallion* shares with Laforgue's pianos the voice, never answered, of invitation and love.

Pound included in *Instigations* a translation of one of the Pierrot poems, and just as Laforgue's Pierrots advance and withdraw in their sophistication, viewing the human scene with a double sense of desire and detachment, so Mauberley, disarmed by his own sensibility, gelded by his own perceptions, withdraws altogether. *Instigations* contains another work of Laforgue's, Pound's rehandling of *Salomé* from *Moralités Légendaires* in which "mousseline" and "enmousselined" are used with almost metronomic regularity in announcing Salomé's arrivals and in describing her costumes. The presence of Pound's "divagation" from Laforgue serves as reminder of the heroes of *Moralités Légendaires*, most specifically of Lohengrin, whom Elsa woos on their wedding night with the first refrain of *Complainte des Pianos*, and who, in the transports of nuptial rapture, embraces his pillow rather than his bride, escaping from a marriage he is incapable of completing when the pillow transforms itself into the beloved Swan and lifts him "vers les altitudes de la Métaphysique de l'Amour, aux glaciers miroirs que nulle haleine de jeune fille ne saurait ternir de buée pour y tracer du doigt son nom avec la date! . . ."

Another relationship between *Mauberley* and *Moralités Légendaires* is that between a descriptive passage in *Le Miracle des Roses* and the sequence's *Medallion*, which, though undoubtedly based on a Luini portrait also echoes the details of

. . . cheveux d'ambre roux massés sur le front et minutieusement tressés en doux chignon plat à la Julia Mammea sur la nuque pure. . . .

Laforgue's essential tone occurs rarely in *Mauberley* after the *Ode*, however. Pound's white remains Gautier's "blanc d'albâtre" rather than Laforgue's "blanc de cold-cream," but the contrasts, the musical pattern of development and variation, do stand in close relation to Laforgue and are early evidence of Pound's application of the Laforguian techniques.

Nevertheless, there is a remaining influence to be investigated. In some ways its neglect parallels the neglect of Gautier; for just as the lack of any primary influence upon Eliot's 1920 poems by Gautier may have obscured the influence of *Émaux et Camées* upon *Mauberley*, so may Eliot's use of Remy de Gourmont in *The Sacred Wood* have placed an emphasis for today's reader on only one part of Gourmont's work.

In both *Instigations* and *Make It New*, the study *Remy de Gourmont A Distinction Followed by Notes* follows immediately the survey of Henry James. In *Make It New* the two are placed together under the joint title *Henry James and Remy de Gourmont*, logically enough, for the first sentences of the Gourmont study read:

The mind of Remy de Gourmont was less like the mind of Henry James than any contemporary mind I can think of. James's drawing of *mœurs contemporaines* was so circumstantial, so concerned with the setting, with detail, nuance, social aroma, that his transcripts were 'out of date' almost before his books had gone into a second edition. . . .

The similarity between the range of Gourmont's work and Pound's is striking. An interest in Provençal poetry, in the later Latin poets, in a studied eroticism, and a willingness to generalize from sometimes slender evidence or even from a single fixed point characterize both men. The Gourmont used by Eliot is a somewhat different Gourmont from the author of the *Épilogues* and *Promenades Littéraires*, from the Gourmont of *Physique de l'Amour* with its vivid account of the virgin mole's flight before her inflamed pursuer, from the Gourmont of the cheerfully erotic collection of stories, *Couleurs*, in which Gourmont, carrying on the vowel-color symbolism of Rimbaud and René Ghil, equates colors with feminine types, each of whom finds her own shade of amorous fulfillment.

It is this second Gourmont who attracted Pound. In his first tribute to him, published in *The Fortnightly Review* (December 1, 1915) and reprinted in *Pavannes and Divisions*, Pound was already celebrating him as one in touch with the younger generation of writers: "He had not lost touch with *les jeunes*." Pound writes enthusiastically of Gourmont's sonnets in prose and praises what Gourmont called "la géometrie subordonnée du corps humain." For *Mauberley* the most important links here are Pound's extractions from Gourmont on this theme:

J'ai plus aimé les yeux que toutes les autres manifestations corporelles de la beauté. . . .

Les yeux sont le manomètre de la machine animale. . . .

and again

Je parlerais des yeux, je chanterais les yeux toute ma vie. Je sais toutes leurs couleurs et toutes leurs volontés, leur destinée. . . .

In a note for *Poetry* (January, 1916) that Pound must have written at about the same time, he again comments on Gourmont's connection with the younger generation and remarks that "Nietzsche has done no harm in France because France has understood that thought can exist apart from action. . . ."

Pound's full study of Gourmont (*Little Review*, February-March, 1919) repeats these points and expands them. The high regard in which Pound held the book that he was to publish a translation of in 1921 under the title *The Natural Philosophy of Love*[11] is shown when he writes:

Physique de l'Amour (1903) should be used as a text-book of biology. Between the biological basis in instinct, and the "Sequaire of Goddes-chalk" in *Le Latin Mystique* (1892) stretch Gourmont's studies of amour and aesthetics.

It is these studies that form one of Pound's chief preoccupations with Gourmont, as an extensive quotation will show:

The emotions are equal before the aesthetic judgment. He does not grant the duality of body and soul, or at least suggests that this mediaeval duality is unsatisfactory; there is an inter-penetration, an osmosis of body and soul, at least for hypothesis.

"My words are the unspoken words of my body."

And in all his exquisite treatment of all emotion he will satisfy many

---

[11] That Pound was already translating the book, or at least considering the problems of translating it, at the time he wrote the *Little Review* article is indicated by his reference to it as Gourmont's "Physiologie de l'Amour" in a note he wrote concerning Frederic Manning's article "M. de Gourmont and the Problem of Beauty."

whom August Strindberg, for egregious example, will not. From the studies of insects to Christine evoked from the thoughts of Diomede, sex is not a monstrosity or an exclusively German study.* And the entire race is not bound to the habits of the *mantis* or of other insects equally melodramatic. Sex, in so far as it is not a purely physiological reproductive mechanism, lies in the domain of aesthetics, the junction of tactile and magnetic senses; as some people have accurate ears both for rhythm and for pitch, and as some are tone deaf, some impervious to rhythmic subtlety and variety, so in this other field of the senses some desire the trivial, some the processional, the stately, the master-work.

As some people are good judges of music, and insensible to painting and sculpture, so the fineness of one sense may entail no corresponding fineness in another, or at least no corresponding critical perception of differences.

Emotions to Henry James were more or less things that other people had and that one didn't go into; at any rate not in drawing rooms. The gods had not visited James, and the Muse, whom he so frequently mentions, appeared doubtless in corsage, the narrow waist, the sleeves puffed at the shoulders, *à la mode* 1890–2.

Here, then, in the contrast drawn between Gourmont and James we see Mauberley as a Jamesian figure, sensitive indeed to painting and sculpture, perceptive of physical detail, but victim of another, and quite basic, kind of "anaesthesis." In a note on one of Gourmont's statements about aesthetics, Pound says: "Each of the senses has its own particular eunuchs." And to make the dissociation of James and Gourmont quite explicit, Pound writes in a single sentence: "In contradiction to, in wholly antipodal distinction from, Henry James, Gourmont was an artist of the nude." It is in such passages, I think, that one begins to sense the fundamental importance of Gourmont to *Mauberley*.

At the same time, one would expect to find in *Mauberley* the sort of immediate trace for Gourmont that has already been

---

* "A German study, Hobson, A German study!" *Tarr*. [Pound's note.]

pointed out for Gautier, Bion, James, and Laforgue. It is contained in the portrait of the modern woman:

> "Conservatrix of Milésien".
> Habits of mind and feeling,
> Possibly. But in Ealing
> With the most bank-clerkly of Englishmen?

Pound provides his own note in the essay, during the course of a survey of Gourmont's books similar to the survey of James's:

> In *Histoires Magiques* (1894): *La Robe Blanche, Yeux d'eau, Marguerite Rouge, Soeur de Sylvie, Danaette,* are all of them special cases, already showing his perception of nevrosis, of hyperaesthesia. His mind is still running on tonal variations in *Les Litanies de la Rose.*
> "Pourtant il y a des yeux aux bout des doigts."
> "Femmes, conservatrices des traditions milésiennes."

Both quotations come from the last story in *Histoires Magiques, Stratagèmes,*[12] and for Mauberley the context of the second is important. The narrator of *Stratagèmes* reviews his successive conquests among women, and after recounting a few early and more or less normal, adventures, he pauses:

> ... Mettre de l'esprit dans la saveur, de l'âme dans le parfum, du sentiment dans le toucher ...
> Désirs, grenades pleines de rubis prisonniers dont un coup de dent fait ruisseler l'éblouissance,—un coup de dent de femme.
> Des femmes, au bon endroit, savent mordre. Elles ne doivent pas être méprisées, ces conservatrices des traditions milésiennes,—mais c'est bien monotone et les artistes sont rares.

It is necessary to stress the sexual connotation here, for Pound early began to use the phrase in a more general sense. Writing to

---

[12] "Pourtant, il y a des yeux au bout des doigts, des yeux de chat faits pour les ténèbres ..." *Stratagèmes* also provided the "nevrosis" of the entry, which Pound apparently insisted upon in both *Instigations* and *Make It New* as against what I take to be the *Little Review* proofreader's "neurosis." "... la contagieuse névrose me gagne ..."

John Quinn about Maud Gonne on November 15, 1918, he said:

The other point M.G. omits from her case is that she went to Ireland without permit and in disguise, in the first place, during war time.

"Conservatrices des traditions Milesiennes," as de Gourmont calls them. There are people who have no sense of the value of "civilization" or public order.

And in his own note to the translation of *Physique de l'Amour*, Pound rephrases the tag in a way that includes both the original sexual sense and his own generalization: "Woman, the conservator, the inheritor of past gestures . . ." That for *Mauberley* the "gestures" are close to Gourmont's original intention is made clear by the remainder of the stanza, the "conservatrix" living with the most bank-clerkly of Englishmen and the "bon endroit" the suburb of Ealing. Certainly she is no "artiste," no stimulus to even the mildest Milesian Tale.

To return, then—Gourmont's immediate presence established—to the passage already quoted in which the music-love theme is sounded. The crucial poem in *Mauberley* to be examined here is the second of the "Mauberley" section, which derives its entire meaning from a music-flower-love symbolism. I have already noted the sexual level of this poem, specifically in connection with the "orchid." On the flower level, the irides wait with opened petals for the "botticellian sprays" of *The Birth of Venus*, in which the entwined male and female zephyrs direct their jets through a curtain of falling flowers. For the detail of this passage, Pound turned to the painting and also to Botticelli's own literary source, Poliziano's *La Giostra*, deriving his "diastasis" of the eyes from two lines describing Cyparissus, however, instead of the Cyprian:

> Bagna Cipresso ancor pel cervio gli occhi
> Con chiome or aspre e già distese e bionde,
>
> (82: 5, 6)

In this picture of Cyparissus' metamorphosis into the cypress, the pair of adjectives "distese e bionde" modify "chiome," as the young man's crown of hair ("chiome" is used here both as "head of hair" and "crown of a tree") is already "divided and yellowish." Pound, seizing on the two words and linking them with "gli occhi" immediately above, translated something like "the wide-spaced and light-colored eyes," which is accurate enough for the painting itself. "La dea Ciprigna" a few stanzas beyond these lines, together with "distesi" used twice in nearby passages, and the "zefiri lascivi" from the actual description of Venus' birth, apparently contributed to this accidental confusion. (It may, on the other hand, be a completely conscious distortion, though this seems doubtful to me.) This indication of the source of Pound's "diastasis" would be highly speculative if he had not with fine economy used the other of the two adjectives in *Canto VII*, applying it to the eye (as if the complete phrase were "occhio biondo") and precisely to the iris of the eye:

> Eyes floating in dry, dark air,
> E biondo, with glass-grey iris, with an even side-fall of hair
> The stiff, still features.

There is every reason to hesitate, however; for despite the emphasis on eyes, there may be an intermediate echo here from Dante:

> . . . e quell' altro ch'è biondo
> È Opizzo da Esti . . .
> (*Inf.* XII, 110, 111)

But even if, ignoring the absence of the accent, one decides to read the phrase in *Canto VII* as "He is fair," the ultimate source still seems to be Poliziano when one finds in *Canto LXXXI*, one of *The Pisan Cantos*, the full phrase used at last:

> Saw but the eyes and stance between the eyes,
> colour, diastasis. . . .

So far as *Mauberley* is concerned, this is simply evidence of the way in which this particular poem is dominated by the image of Venus.

Pound's memory was probably ranging back over a number of years, for the only other indication in his work that he had read *La Giostra*, beyond a passing reference to Poliziano in *The Spirit of Romance*, occurs in the first version of *Canto I*, published in *Poetry* for April, 1917. Here, as in *Mauberley*, he is writing specifically of *The Birth of Venus* and Botticelli's use of Simonetta de Vespucci, whose favor Giuliano de Medici had won as victor of the tournament the poem celebrated:

> How many worlds we have! If Botticelli
> Brings her ashore on that great cockle-shell—
> His Venus (Simonetta?),
> And Spring and Aufidus fill all the air
> With their clear-outlined blossoms?
> World enough.

To return once more to Gourmont, the one poem of his that Pound quoted in "A Study in French Poets" was *Litanies de la Rose*, of which Pound wrote: "The procession of all beautiful women moves before one in the 'Litanies de la Rose'; and the rhythm is incomparable." For *Mauberley*, two of Gourmont's roses are of particular importance, the first for the "tea-rose tea-gown . . . mousseline of Cos" passage, the second for the poem under immediate discussion:

> Rose rose, pucelle au cœur désordonné, rose rose, robe de mousseline, entr'ouvre tes ailes fausses, ange, fleur hypocrite, fleur du silence.

> Rose bleue, rose iridine, monstre couleur des yeux de la Chimère, rose bleue, lève un peu tes paupières: as-tu peur qu'on te regarde, les yeux dans les yeux, Chimère, fleur hypocrite, fleur du silence!

Here, and in many other passages from Gourmont appears his insistence on flower symbolism, and in "rose iridine" lies the probable clue to Pound's use of the "irides" as a double flower-eye image. One would expect to find somewhere in Gourmont's work the conjunction of orchid and iris with a sexual connotation to complete the pattern, but Pound picked up this hint from another source. *Instigations* includes what Pound identifies no more specifically than a translation "from an eighteenth-century author," entitled *Genesis, or the First Book in the Bible.* This translation, which originally appeared in the *Little Review* (November, 1918), is a translation of the entry *Genèse* in Voltaire's *Dictionnaire Philosophique,* and in the course of it Voltaire, discussing the sons of the gods who found the daughters of earth fair, comments: "There is no race, except perhaps the Chinese, which has not recorded gods getting young girls with child." Pound adds his own note to this:

In Fenollosa's notes on Kutsugen's[13] ode to "Sir in the Clouds," I am unable to make out whether the girl is more than a priestess. She bathes in hot water made fragrant by boiling orchids in it, she washes her hair and binds iris into it, she puts on the dress of flowery colors, and the god illimitable in his brilliance descends; she continues her attention to her toilet, in very reverent manner.

Pound had used flowers as sexual symbols long before this, specifically in the poem *Coitus* (entitled *Pervigilium* in *Lustra*), which opens:

> The gilded phaloi of the crocuses
> are thrusting at the spring air.

And later, in *Moeurs Contemporaines*:

> You enter and pass hall after hall,
> Conservatory follows conservatory,
> Lilies lift their white symbolical cups,
> Whence their symbolical pollen has been excerpted.

---

[13] Kutsugen is the Japanese form of Ch'ü Yüan. Pound's *Cathay*, founded on Fenollosa's notes, has produced a rash of references to "the Chinese poet Rihaku," or "Omakitsu," or "Kakuhaku." There is surely no reason to retain these Japanese forms instead of using the standard romanized spelling of the poets' actual Chinese names: Li Po, Wang Wei, and Kuo P'u in these three instances.

With this flower-music-sex theme in mind, one should turn to examine the separate epigraph of the second "Mauberley" poem:

"Qu'est ce qu'ils savent de l'amour, et qu'est ce qu'ils peuvent comprendre?

S'ils ne comprennent pas la poésie, s'ils ne sentent pas la musique, qu'est ce qu'ils peuvent comprendre de cette passion en comparaison avec laquelle la rose est grossière et le parfum des violettes un tonnerre?" CAID ALI

As I have already noted, Pound has written to Kimon Friar that "Caid Ali" is his own pseudonym. I assume it was chosen in salute to the part played by floral figures in the elaborate erotic symbolism of Persian poetry, with, perhaps, a bow in the direction of the *Rubaiyat*. At the same time, one recognizes immediately the reflection of Gourmont, in tone, in the flowers, in the rhetorical questions,[14] and one suspects that somewhere in this aesthetic bouquet must lurk a specifically sexual reference beyond the mention of "amour." The "grossness" of the rose suggests it, and the reader of *Physique de l'Amour* in Pound's translation recognizes its full statement instantly in "un tonnerre." Twice in *The Natural Philosophy of Love* Pound uses "thunder-clap" to describe the sexual climax (of the bull!), once to translate Gourmont's "éclair" and again to translate "foudre." The full irony of the epigraph in relation to Mauberley's "fundamental passion" and his "anæsthesis" is not revealed without this clue.

With it, the underlying theme and the underlying musical structure of *Mauberley* are apparent. The musical development takes the form of what might be called a double counterpoint, or a major and minor counterpoint. In the "eye" passages from Gourmont and his "unspoken words of my body" one sees

[14] For comparison, one might cite an example from Gourmont's notice of Octave Uzanne's *Le Célibat et l'Amour*: "C'est une philosophie colorée par le rêve, car où mettrait-on du rêve, si on n'en mettrait dans l'amour?"

Pound's source of the minor counterpoint, and simply to trace the series of eye-images reveals much of the method: *inward gaze—quick eyes gone under earth's lid—all of Yeux Glauques—skylike limpid eyes—eye-lid and cheek-bone—irides—diastasis—if her colour came against his gaze—the eyes turn topaz.* The fullest series, however, and the one that displays the method at its most effective level of variation is made up of mouth-images: *trout for factitious bait—accelerated grimace—an old bitch gone in the teeth—charm, smiling at the good mouth—*all the references in *Envoi,* particularly *some other mouth—firmness, not the full smile—mouths biting empty air (Vacuos exercet [in] aera morsus)—unfit as the red-beaked steeds of the Cytheræan for a chain bit—the faint susurrus of his subjective hosannah—the grand piano utters a profane protest with her clear soprano.* The same method produces the balance between "the elegance of Circe's hair" in the *Ode* and the "basket-work of braids" in the *Medallion,* the latter an echo of the "Minoan undulation" that strengthened Mauberley's hopes for a time.

This minor counterpoint is implicit in the major counterpoint: the severe and exact balance maintained between the poems in the first section dominated by Pound and the poems in the second section dominated by Mauberley. The first statement of the suite sounds this with

> For three years, out of key with his time
> He strove

answered in the "Mauberley" section by

> For three years, diabolus in the scale,[15]
> He drank ambrosia.

---

[15] "The devil in music" is the augmented fourth, which gave the medieval musicians great difficulty and gave rise to the tag:

> *Mi contra Fa*
> *Diabolus in musica.*

I take it to be pure coincidence that Hugh Selwyn Mauberley's initials are the same as His Satannic Majesty's, but considering the association

Whereas Pound's reaction to what the age demands is a scathing and agile denunciation of the modern world leading him to his first attack on usury, Mauberley lacks agility and at the sight of beauty he makes "no immediate application / Of this to relation of the state." Pound's subjective and active crowning of himself with Daphne's laurel is set against "the faint susurrus" of Mauberley's "subjective hosannah."

The most telling contrast in this major counterpoint is a sexual one, with the "phallic and ambrosial" of the first section diminished to the purely "ambrosial circumstances" of the second. Even the intermediate poems, the "contacts" of the two men, share this theme. Both the pre-Raphaelite and the Nineties sections echo it in terms of sexual frustration. The stylist can enjoy only an "uneducated mistress" as against the "conservatrix of Milésien" and the final sterility of the Lady Valentine's and the Lady Jane's circles. The inadequacy of the age is embodied in the eunuch who rules over it; its victims do not know the faun's flesh; they have the vote instead of the religio-sexual rite of circumcision.

It is with this contrast in mind that one must examine the portrait of Mauberley as it is revealed beneath the surface gravity, the mild objectivity and sympathy of the Jamesian observer. The most obvious contrast here is the balancing of the *Envoi* against the *Medallion.* The two poems handle the same scene, but whereas the poet of the *Envoi*, working from Waller's *Go, Lovely Rose*, writes a poem that echoes down the entire line of the English poets, most specifically Shakespeare with

> One substance and one colour
> Braving time,

---

of Joyce and Pound at this time, it is a point worth passing mention. In the same doubtful area is the possibility of "Mauberley," the name, apparently a lavender extension of "Moberly," being derived from Brigadier Hugh Stephenson Moberly (1873–1947) and even connected with the folk-saying "Always too late like Mobberly clock."

and implies throughout an invitation to active passion, the poet
of the *Medallion* scrupulously notes each detail of the scene, not
recognizing the invitation of the song beyond the grand piano's
"profane protest," not seeing in "the gold-yellow frock" the
color of Hymen, not finding a living Venus but a reminder of
Reinach's *Apollo*, and closing with a careful "scientific" record
of the inviting eyes as they turn topaz beneath the half-watt rays
of the final star-lit night. To emphasize this quality of the
Medallion one can turn to *Canto V*, where the same nexus of
music, topaz, the Hymeneal color, and the star Hesperus (νυκτὸς
ἄγαλμα) is used with the full implication of active passion, "The
bride awaiting the god's touch":

> Topaz I manage, and three sorts of blue;
>   but on the barb of time.
> The fire? always, and the vision always,
> Ear dull, perhaps, with the vision, flitting
> And fading at will. Weaving with points of gold,
> Gold-yellow, saffron . . . The roman shoe, Aurunculeia's
> And come shuffling feet, and cries "Da nuces!
> "Nuces!" praise, and Hymenaeus "brings the girl to
>   her man"
> Or "here Sextus had seen her."
> Titter of sound about me, always.
>   and from "Hesperus . . ."
> Hush of the older song: "Fades light from sea-crest,
> "And in Lydia walks with pair'd women
> "Peerless among the pairs, that once in Sardis
> "In satieties . . ."[16]

With this ironic revelation of Mauberley's inadequacy in
mind, and remembering the implications of "un tonnerre" in
the Caid Ali epigraph, one can turn back to the first "Mauber-
ley" poem and see that it announces with ribald frankness this
entire theme, but announces it so blatantly that it is almost
automatically overlooked. The first stanza of the poem suggests

---

[16] The principal bases here are Catullus and Sappho.

it, with Mauberley turning from the etching to the severe head of the insatiable empress, and the bald announcement follows with

> "His true Penelope
> Was Flaubert,"
> And his tool
> The engraver's.

It is particularly bald when one recalls Gautier's reference to "la roue du graveur."

Here one must turn to Pound's own note appended to his translation of *Physique de l'Amour*. Gourmont advances his personal theories of intellectual fecundation, saying, as translated by Pound:

> Virgin-birth might establish itself. Certain males could be born in each century, as happens in the intellectual order, and they could fecundate the generation of loins, as genius fecundates the generation of minds.

From this passage in Gourmont and from some of Gourmont's remarks on the sexual mechanism of vertebrates Pound developed his note, in which he elaborates on his own intuitive theory of the human brain as "a clot of genital fluid":

> There are traces of it [this theory] in the symbolism of phallic religions, man really the phallus or spermatozoid charging, head-on, the female chaos; integration of the male in the male organ. Even oneself has felt it, driving any new idea into the great passive vulva of London, a sensation analagous to the male feeling in copulation.

Not only is *Mauberley* Pound's farewell to London; it contains in itself a definition of the "female chaos" that now rejected or ignored the pressure of his advances. For Pound characterizes the ultimate dissolution of the age after the War as "hysterias, trench confessions, laughter out of dead bellies," in which "hysteria," like Mauberley's "orchid," uses the full power of its Greek root, ὑστέρα (womb) to reveal the new, "female" formlessness.

Yet if the second stanza of the first "Mauberley" poem is actually the ribald declaration that it now appears to be, one would expect to find some balance for it in the first section, preferably in the *Ode*, just as the first two lines of the stanza come from the *Ode*. The balancing line is there, with a sort of sixth-form wild sexual humor about it, in a statement far more ribald than its "Mauberley" echo. The line is "Bent resolutely on wringing lilies from the acorn," and to read it fully one must remember that just as "orchid" is ὄρχις, and just as "hysteria" is ὑστέρα, so is "acorn" *glans* in Latin and *gland* in French. Thus what appears to be a proverbial, almost a Biblical expression—*Do men gather figs of thistles? Can the fig tree bear olive berries?*—is actually a raucous echo of the sort of humor that had always delighted Pound in Catullus and Ovid and had led him to write lines like those that open *Fratres Minores*:

> With minds still hovering above their testicles
> Certain poets here and in France
> Still sigh over established and natural fact
> Long since fully discussed by Ovid.

Though the glandular implications of the line from the *Ode* seem clear enough, it is possible to go farther and indicate where Pound picked up the suggestion for it in *Physique de l'Amour*. The sentence reads, and again in his own translation:

The gland, which takes all intermediate forms between ball and point, has in the rhinocerus the shape of a gross fleur-de-lis.[17]

Only after an exploration of all these images can one place beside the eye and mouth images—the musical series itself, from the sirens' song to the song of the *Medallion* is worth equal attention—the final, sexual series on which *Mauberley* rests.

---

[17] The original may be of interest here for its use of "grossière," which occurs also in the Caid Ali passage. "Le gland, qui affecte toutes les formes intermédiaires entre la boule et la pointe, prend, chez le rhinocéros, celle d'une grossière fleur de lys."

But if this is the final level on which *Mauberley* is to be read, one is struck by the disparity between the astonishing complexity of its surface and the apparent simplicity of its base, a disparity that comes close to being disconcerting. R. P. Blackmur is, I think, treating this problem when he writes of *Mauberley* in *The Double Agent*:

What we see is Mr. Pound fitting his substance with a surface; he is a craftsman, and we are meant to appreciate his workmanship. When we try to discern the substance, we find that the emphasis on craft has produced a curious result. Instead of the poem being, as with most poets of similar dimensions, a particularised instance of a plot, myth, attitude, or convention, with Mr. Pound movement is in the opposite direction; the poem flows into the medium and is lost in it, like water in sand.

I find it difficult to believe that the "substance" of *Mauberley* even at this level, once discerned, is altogether swallowed up by the medium, but that the relationship between substance and surface here presents difficulties is, I think, undeniable.

Actually, however, Pound is trying to do far more than simply exercise what Marianne Moore was later to call his over-emphasis on "unprudery" or merely assert the greater complete-ness of the complete man over the incomplete. Once again, the study of Gourmont gives the key, not only to *Mauberley* but also to Pound's *Propertius*:

If in Diomède we find an Epicurean receptivity, a certain aloofness, an observation of contacts and auditions, in contrast to the Propertian attitude:

Ingenium nobis ipsa puella facit,

this is perhaps balanced by

"Sans vous, je crois bien que je n'aimerais plus beaucoup et que je n'aurais plus une extrême confiance ni dans la vie ni moi-même." (In "Lettres à l'Amazone.")

But there is nothing more unsatisfactory than saying that De Gour-mont "had such and such ideas" or held "such and such views," the thing is that he held ideas, intuitions, perceptions in a certain personal exquisite manner. In a criticism of him, "criticism" being an over violent word, in, let us say, an indication of him, one wants merely to show that one has oneself made certain dissociations; as here, between the æsthetic receptivity of tactile and magnetic values, of the perception of beauty in these relationships, and the conception of love, passion, emotion as an intellectual instigation; such as Propertius claims it; such as we find it declared in the King of Navarre's

"De fine amor vient science et beauté";

and constantly in the troubadours.

Here, then, is *Mauberley*'s base, expressed through Pound's own dissociation of ideas in Gourmont's work. The dissociation is precisely the dissociation Pound makes between the Muses of Gourmont and James; it is the structural dissociation made between the two parts of *Hugh Selwyn Mauberley* as a composition; it is the dissociation made between Pound, the poet of "love, passion, emotion as an intellectual instigation," and Mauberley, the poet of "aesthetic receptivity of tactile and magnetic values, of the perception of beauty in these relationships."

Perhaps it is anticlimactic to insist that a problem still remains, the problem of what one might call the "exterior" relationship between Hugh Selwyn Mauberley and Ezra Pound. For *Mauberley* taken entirely on its own terms, the relation is, I think, clear enough: the passive aesthete played off against the active instigator. But perhaps even those who feel that a poet's biography has no part in a reading of his works will admit that the presence of *E. P.* in the title of the *Ode* may excuse brief consideration of issues outside the strict limits of the poem.

In the "Autobiography" prefixed to the New Directions *Selected Poems* Pound writes: "1918 began investigation of causes of war, to oppose same." The importance of this to *Mauberley* is its indication that at the close of the war Pound was moving toward what he was eventually to call his "renunciation of poetry for politics." That the Pound of *The Oxford Book of Victorian Verse* was already a figure of the past seems clear, but it is hardly satisfactory to follow custom and look upon Mauberley as a mask of Pound's own early aesthetic focus; for Pound's allegiances here were always with those who, however hampered by the age and their own limitations, did, in Pound's judgment, play their roles as instigators: Swinburne and Rossetti, Dowson and Johnson. What is, perhaps, useful and pertinent is to suggest that in the person of Mauberley Pound was rejecting—though it is always necessary to insist that this is altogether outside the limits of the poem and in no sense on a personal level—a mask of what he feared to become as an artist by remaining in England.

6 notes of varying length

On the basis of the preceding explorations it is possible to give a somewhat fuller reading of *Mauberley* than the outline set down earlier. In the notes that follow, however, I have not attempted to repeat or summarize what I have already written of the influence of Gautier, Bion, James, Laforgue, and Gourmont, and the scattered comments after the brief paraphrase of each poem are intended only to touch on points not already dealt with.

HUGH SELWYN MAUBERLEY
(LIFE AND CONTACTS)
"VOCAT AESTUS IN UMBRAM"
NEMESIANUS Ec. IV.

Although the parody "life and letters" parenthesis and the epigraph from Nemesianus ("The heat calls us into the shade") have disappeared in the most recent text of *Mauberley*, they are perhaps still worth a few comments. Both appear to be bits of baroque plasterwork for *Mauberley*'s façade, of use when the sequence originally came out as a separate book, or, later, as an independent section of a book with its own title page, but of little further significance than this. To read into the line from Nemesianus more than a retreat from the full sun of the day parallel to Hugh Selwyn Mauberley's withdrawal from the world is probably not of much use. Friar finds here "the note of exile"; but Nemesianus was a native of Carthage and not a Roman exile. Richard A. Long's contention (*Explicator*, June, 1952) that the quotation from a Latin poet of the Silver Age suggests the dividing line between "eras of sunlight and shadow in the practice of letters" seems to me to put too much weight on the epigraph, and to ignore Pound's own pattern of classic values.

E. P. ODE POUR L'ELECTION DE SON SEPULCHRE

Adapting Ronsard's title *De l'Élection de son Sepulchre* (*Odes*, IV, 4), Pound writes his own epitaph, revealing both his critics' view of his career and his own view of it. The basic theme is the portrait of the poet as Odysseus, who has heard the Sirens' song (*"Ἴδμεν γάρ τοι πάνθ', ὅσ' ἐνὶ Τροίῃ*, "For we know all the things that are in Troy," *Odyssey*, XII, 189), who has fished by the "obstinate isles" of his voyage (Pound's studies, as noted by Leavis, in Provençal, Anglo-Saxon, Chinese and Japanese, Greek, Latin, Italian and French, but also the stubborn island he is preparing to leave, as Kenner points out), whose "true Penelope was Flaubert" not only in his search for exact expression but also in his effort to expose the stupidity of accepted ideas, and who prefers to admire and actively love beauty for itself however dangerous ("Circe's hair") rather than applaud the banalities inscribed on sundials or the clichés of public action summarized by "the march of events." Pound records his birth in a foreign, "half-savage" land, and reinforces his irony by using the first line of Villon's *Grand Testament* for a tag as the age dismisses him as no credit to the Muses.

A pair of images, equating himself first with Capaneus, one of the Seven against Thebes, struck down by Zeus on the city wall for his impiety and later joined in death on the funeral pyre by his wife Evadne, and second with a trout rising to take an illusionary lure, mark the limits of the terms in which Pound and the age refer to their subject.

The first line, "For three years out of key with his time," and the line, "Bent resolutely on wringing lilies from the acorn," sound the music-flower-sex note in two scales: one the musical form of the poem, the other the theme of active passion with its grace notes of ribaldry.

II

The voice of the man so summarily and condescendingly dismissed in the *Ode* now answers the criticism of "his time" by beginning to characterize the age itself, denouncing its false values, its narcissism, its rejection of the classics even in paraphrase (Pound's own work, with his *Homage to Sextus Propertius* probably the chief reference), and its preference for mere movement over the "sculpture" of lasting beauty.

III

Pound enters into an itemized account of his denunciation, contrasting the modern degeneracy with the classic ideal. The fashionable tea-gown is now favored over the Propertian tunic of Coan silk; Sappho's lyre is replaced by a mechanical piano; the phallic and ambrosial rites of Dionysus have given way to the maceration of Christianity; The Beautiful ($\tau\grave{o}$ $\kappa\alpha\lambda\grave{o}\nu$) is judged purely by its money value in the market. Rephrasing a line from Pindar's *Second Olympian Ode* ($\tau\acute{\iota}\nu\alpha$ $\theta\epsilon\acute{o}\nu$, $\tau\acute{\iota}\nu'\ddot{\eta}\rho\omega\alpha$, $\tau\acute{\iota}\nu\alpha$ $\delta'\ddot{\alpha}\nu\delta\rho\alpha$ $\kappa\epsilon\lambda\alpha\delta\acute{\eta}\sigma\omega\mu\epsilon\nu$; "what god, what hero, what man shall we praise?") Pound savagely echoes the $\tau\acute{\iota}\nu'$, $\tau\acute{\iota}\nu'$, $\tau\acute{\iota}\nu\alpha$ in his "tin wreath," finding no one worthy.

* * *

Perhaps it is not out of place to note that in the line "Even the Christian beauty" the stress falls on "beauty" and not on

"Christian." Although τὸ καλὸν is used in this poem in its primary sense of "The Beautiful," it is more closely related in Pound's thinking to the political theme that follows than one might suspect, since beauty and order of all kinds stand for him almost as identities. A passage near the end of *Jefferson and/or Mussolini* (written in 1933) illustrates this:

> Towards which I assert again my own firm belief that the Duce will stand not with despots and the lovers of power but with the lovers of
> ORDER
> τὸ καλὸν

Pound used the phrase much earlier with similar connotations, though here purely in an aesthetic sense, when he wrote in *Patria Mia* (written in 1912) on a theme closely related to parts of *Mauberley*:

> I don't mean that the American is any less sensitive to the love of precision, or to τὸ καλὸν than is the young lady in English society. He is simply so much farther removed from the sources, from the few dynamic people who really know good from bad; even when the good is not conventional; even when the good is not freakish.
>
> It has been well said of the "lady in society" that art criticism is one of her functions. She babbles of it as of "the play," or of hockey, or of "town topics." She believes in catholicity of taste, in admiring no one thing more than anything else. But she is not ubiquitous. Even in London one may escape from her paths and by-ways.

The use of Sappho and Pindar in the same poem is not accidental. Writing to Iris Barry in July, 1916, Pound said: "They all go on gassing about the 'deathless voice' and the 'Theban eagle' as if Pindar wasn't the prize wind-bag of all ages. *The* 'bass-drum,' etc." Returning to the subject the following month he wrote her: "And there is the gulph between TIS O SAPPHO ADIKEI, and Pindar's big rhetorical drum TINA THEON, TIN' EROA, TINA D'ANDREA KELADESOMEN, which one should get carefully fixed in the mind." Earlier (1915) he had written Harriet Monroe, discussing her notions of suitable "models" to be followed by younger writers: "I don't think Pindar any safer than Poe. 'Theban Eagle' be blowed. A dam'd rhetorician half the time." Pound's series of comments on a number of classical writers came out in *The Egoist* during the time he was writing *Mauberley*, and in the March-April, 1919, number he returns to the attack, the reference to the Ἀναξιφόρμιγγες ὕμνοι making particularly interesting reading, since it is the first line of the *Second Olympian* and is of importance to the opening of *Canto IV*. Pound wrote:

Pindar is a *pompier*, and his Ἀναξιφόρμιγγες ὕμνοι etc., ought to be sent to the dust-bin along with Shelley's *Sensitive Plant*. The harm done by pedants yapping about the glory that was this and the grandeur that was the other; telling impressionable small boys that all Greek is literature and all Latin is jurisprudential, is incalculable. . . . I know as the merest of minor details that my prose was held back three years because I had read some gush of MacKail's over Tacitus.

Pound's distaste for the "big rhetorical drum" is still with him when he writes to W. H. D. Rouse in May, 1937: "Also you can *not* sell me Pindar, and you can't sell me a dialect that never was spoken and never will be. . . . I will back you and Homer in any international Olympiad, but I won't be loaded up with Mr. Pindar." Pindar's line is probably rehandled only in the interests of the rhyme and the heavy opening beats on τίν', and the implication is that not even Pindar could find anyone to crown. One suspects that had Capaneus-Sthenelus-Pound been in at the final sack of Thebes, *no* house would have been left standing.

IV

The climax of modern stupidity is the sacrifice of youth in the World War. Those who are not killed return to a society corrupted by usury and hypocrisy, to a chaos of hysteria and formless self-expression.

*   *   *

"Pro domo, in any case . . ." with a nod in the direction

of Cicero's *Pro domo sua* heralds the tags from the Horatian *Dulce et decorum est pro patria mori* ("It is sweet and fitting to die for one's own country," *Carm.*, III, ii, 13). Pound is, by his own standards, as hard on Horace as he is on Pindar in *The Egoist*:

Horace was "the first Parnassien," or the first Royal Academy. He is better than Samain or Heredia. I question if he was as good a poet as Gautier. He was as good as Lionel Johnson.

Because of the association of Horace and Lionel Johnson in Pound's mind it is not altogether fantastic to suggest that Pound may be indicating more than simply "for the home" in his "pro domo." Pound had collected and edited Johnson's poems for Elkin Mathews in 1915. Johnson, a Wykhamite, refers nostalgically a number of times to his school days, particularly to the Winchester institution of Domum Day; "Pro domo" consequently may have had for Pound something of the "old school tie" spirit underlying its surface meaning.

Though "usury age-old and age-thick" appears to be an image of incrustation, Pound may already be using "thick" here as he does in the later Cantos. In a remarkable declaration to Carlo Izzo, his Italian translator, Pound wrote in 1938:

"With Usura the line grows thick"—means the *line* in painting and design. Quattrocento painters still in morally clean era when usury and buggary were on a par. As the moral sense becomes as incapable of moral distinction as the ....p of ....y or ...t ....n or ....n, painting gets bitched. I can tell the bank rate and component of tolerance for usury in any epoch by the quality of *line* in painting. Baroque, etc., era of usury becoming tolerated.

V

Pound writes a final epitaph for the dead, contrasting the sacrifice of young, living flesh with the "old bitch gone in the teeth," the "civilization" which, since it is no longer a functioning unit and is diseased, is nothing but "broken statues" and "battered books."

* * *

In *Jefferson and/or Mussolini*, Pound makes clear that he thoroughly admired Britain's effort in the First World War:

I have seen several admirable shows in my time. I saw groggy old England get up onto her feet from 1914 to '18. I don't like wars, etc. . . . but given the state of decadence and comfort and general incompetence of pre-War England, nobody who saw that effort can remain without respect for England-during-that-war.

I am not contradicting myself. Respect for that honest heave and effort had nothing to do with the state of utter dithering deliquescence into which England slopped in 1919.

YEUX GLAUQUES

Beginning his analysis of the artist's defeat in England at the hands of "knaves," "eunuchs," and "liars," Pound writes of the pre-Raphaelite period, recording the respect given Gladstone and Ruskin as against the abuse of Swinburne and Rossetti. The central portrait here, as noted by Friar, is based on Elizabeth Eleanor Siddal, a popular model for the pre-Raphaelite painters, who became Rossetti's wife, and later died by her own hand. Pound directs his scorn at Robert Williams Buchanan's attack, "The Fleshly School of Poetry" (*Contemporary Review*, October 18, 1871), in the course of which Buchanan singled out Rossetti's "Jenny" as particularly offensive. The poem is an account of an evening spent by a young man in reflection as the head of Jenny, a weary prostitute, rests on his knee. The poem's epigraph is drawn from *The Merry Wives of Windsor* (IV, i, 64), though, as the brackets below indicate, Rossetti did not quote the speech entire:

> Vengeance of Jenny's case! Fie on her! Never
> name her, child [, if she be a whore]!
>
> (Mrs. Quickly)

In some measure equating Elizabeth Siddal and Jenny, though quite without any biographical basis, Pound creates a pre-Raphaelite Muse, echoes his "faun's flesh" of the third poem, and notes that Elizabeth Siddal's eyes occur in the Burne-Jones drawings and in his *Cophetua and the Beggar Maid*, which hangs in the Tate Gallery—although in fact she was not the model used by the artist.

*　　*　　*

Pound's admiration for the *Rubaiyat*, "still-born" until it was discovered by Rossetti (himself the author of a sonnet entitled "Stillborn Love" in *The House of Life*), is based not only on the poem for itself but also because it is a part of the necessary foreign "injection" into the stream of insular British verse. The same element influenced Pound's judgment of Swinburne. Reviewing Gosse's *Life of Swinburne* in an article entitled "Swinburne versus Biographers" (*Poetry*, March, 1918), he wrote: "The Villon translations stand with Rossetti's and the *Rubaiyat* among the Victorian translations," and he classed Swinburne with Browning as being "the best of the Victorian era." Pound's preoccupation at the time with the theme of personal independence, as revealed in his comments on James, is also apparent here. "The passion not merely for political, but also for personal, liberty is the bedrock of Swinburne's writing." At the same time he cannot resist the opportunity of another jibe at Swinburne's rhythms, and just as in the article on the French poets, his target is *Dolores*: "The sound of *Dolores* is in places like that of horses' hoofs being pulled out of mud."

"*SIENA MI FE'; DISFECEMI MAREMMA*"

Moving on to the Nineties, Pound takes the memories of Victor Gustave Plarr as his focus, using as title a line from Dante ("Siena made me, Maremma undid me," *Purg.* V, 135), echoing in it Plarr's foreign birth (in Strasbourg) and the family's removal to Britain after the Franco-Prussian war. Dante's line is spoken by Pia de' Tolomei of Siena, whose husband, in order to marry another woman, either murdered her or had her murdered in Pietra, his castle in the Tuscan Maremma.

Here the two poets who stand out against the background of diffuse mediocrity are Ernest Dowson and Lionel Johnson, who shared Catholicism, alcoholism, and a veneration for Propertius. Johnson died of a fall, not in a pub, but on Fleet Street, and the autopsy revealed that he had never matured physically. As already noted, Pound had edited the *Poetical Works of Lionel Johnson*. The first issue of the first edition contained an introductory essay by Pound that included some of Johnson's judgments of his contemporaries (originally published in the *Dublin Review*), some of whom were still living, and caused the issue's almost immediate withdrawal. As reissued, nothing indicates Pound's part in the work. Some of the comments by Johnson remain interesting. Of Le Gallienne: "A persistent note of—not vulgarity, nor bad taste—but of unconscious familiarity in a bad sense. He belittles things by his touch." Of Symons: "Baudelaire and Verlaine generally ring true. . . . Symons no more does that than a teapot. 'This girl met me in the Haymarket, with a straw hat and a brown paper parcel, and the rest was a delirious delight: that girl I met outside a music hall, we had champagne, and the rest was an ecstasy of shame.' That is Symons." And later: "You might mention Dowson and Victor Plarr as men sure to be successful when their first books appear: Dowson you appreciate, I know: but Plarr is delightful, a kind of half-French, half-Celtic Dobson with nature and the past and dying traditions and wild races for his theme." Pound's preface is chiefly interesting for *Mauberley* in the comparison he draws between Gautier and Johnson, whom he praises for his "neatness and hardness" and lack of amateurism. "In the midst of enthusiasms one thinks perhaps that, if Gautier had not written, Johnson's work might even take its place in Weltliteratur, that it might stand for this clearness and neatness."

I have already noted that Plarr was Librarian to the Royal College of Surgeons and that Pound's opening lines are primarily simple physical description. Plarr had belonged to the Rhymers' Club, his fellow-members being John Davidson, Ernest Dowson, Edwin J. Ellis, George Arthur Greene, Lionel Johnson, Arthur Cecil Hillier, Richard Le Gallienne, Ernest Radford, Ernest Rhys, Thomas William Rolleston, Arthur Symons, John Todhunter, and William Butler Yeats. Pound reviewed Plarr's *Ernest Dowson* (London, 1914) for *Poetry* (April, 1915), referring to Plarr's book of verse (originally planned as a joint publication by Dowson and Plarr) as *The Dorian Mood*, just as he does in *Mauberley*, indicating that he was probably not consciously shortening the full title, *In the Dorian Mood*. Commenting on Dowson himself, Pound wrote: "I have never been disappointed in a man whose work had first drawn me to him." And of Plarr's book he said: "In any case no one who loves his Dowson will go without this memoir. . . ."

The quality of Plarr's reminiscences and the fascination they held for Pound are best illustrated by annotating the poem from the pages of Plarr's *Dowson*, particularly since Pound himself is mentioned in it.

The Battle of Sedan, where Galliffet led his brigade of the Chasseurs d'Afrique in a brilliant but unsupported cavalry charge:

"Sedan!" how well the baby's father [i.e. Victor Plarr] and aunt had had that word driven into their childish brains when, as little creatures, in a beautiful wild forest near Sant Odile in the Vosges, they saw one of their elders stop to talk to two ragged wayworn men in blouses, sitting by the side of the path. Men were these who rested dejectedly, with drooping heads and hanging arms. They brought news of Sedan! They could not believe the things they told.

An hour afterwards all the old brown gnarled hands at the Convent of Saint Odile were being wrung by refugee peasants, by nuns and monks who had been peasants in their mundane time! Down there, down there, in the far vine-clad plain with its Frankish memories, the plain of Alsace, where Guttenberg discovered his *prelum* in the wine-press, among the villages with their romanesque archways and fountains, their ancient steep-roofed houses and yokes of plump somnolent cream-coloured oxen, the dreadful Prussian, who ate queer food and had such unbred manners, would soon set his heavy-booted foot!

Ernest Dowson and Lionel Johnson:

I remember, in horrible Fleet Street days—Fleet Street is, of course, quite different now—shortly before Dowson's letter was written to me. . . .

* * * *

Young Mr Pound, to whom Dowson is a kind of classical myth, just as the ancients are a myth to us all, tells me a story, told him in turn by a good recorder, of how Dowson went to see poor Wilde in Dieppe after the *débâcle*, and how he endeavoured to reform his morality by diverting it at least into a natural channel. It is at best a smoking-room anecdote, not fit for exact repetition. I suppose they drank absinthe together in a big tawdry noisy cafe near the queer odoriferous fish-market where they sell all the monsters of the sea which English fishermen reject.

* * * *

Ernest Dowson is numbered by Mr Holbrook Jackson, in his admirable if somewhat mytho-poetical record of the "Eighteen Nineties," among the interesting band, including Wilde, Beardsley, and Johnson, who joined the Church of Rome in what we now consider the period of "the Decadence."

Lionel Johnson, at least, could give chapter and verse for his conversion. Hardly so Dowson. I shall never forget the day of his admittance to the Church. He came to me rather excitedly, and yet shook hands with weak indecision. His hesitating hand-shake, alas! always betrayed a sorrowful fatigue.

"I have been admitted," he said, but he seemed disappointed, for the heavens had not fallen, nor had a sign been vouchsafed. The priest who had admitted him had done so quite casually and had seemed bored.

Selwyn Image and Stewart Headlam:

The sacred house, about which a volume might be written, had, from about the year 1891, been the home of the *Hobby Horse* writers, and of at least one outsider. My dear friend Professor Selwyn Image still lives there, and will he forgive me if I remind him that the house was at one time referred to as "Fitzroy" and that "Fitzroy" was a movement, an influence, a glory? There were several Fitzroy institutions—notably what was known as "Fitzroy silence" at our austere dinners and lunches. Lionel Johnson, when I left "Fitzroy," declared that it became full of strong mysterious men, who clamoured for large chops and steaks at meals. They are probably very eminent persons by this time.

The original dwellers in "Fitzroy," before my time, were Mr Herbert Horne, who with Professor, then Mr Selwyn Image, edited *The Hobby Horse*, Mr Galton, editor of Matthew Arnold and Lionel Johnson, Mr Arthur Macmurdo, and Lionel Johnson himself. Professor Image at that time kept a studio there, as did the late Mr Machlachlan the landscapist. Mr Randall Davies studied design under Mr Macmurdo and the late Hubert Crackanthorpe was for a time a pupil of Professor Image. Numbers of other distinguished people visited this artistic colony. The list of them would include Mr Mortimer Menpes, Mr Frank Brangwyn (a constant visitor), Mr Walter Crane, the late Oscar Wilde, Mr Dolmetsch, Mr Ernest Rhys, Mr W. B. Yeats, Mr Will. Rothenstein, Father John Gray, the Rev. Stewart Headlam, and a host more. Ernest Dowson had lunched there in the earliest days and had made me emulous to enter the sacred precincts. As a later member of "Fitzroy," in succession to Mr Galton, I had the honour of introducing our foreign discoverer, M. George Olivier Destree, then editor of *La Jeune Belgique*, and now Father Bruno, into the charmed circle.

. . .

The next letter, dated in January, 1893, begins a prolific epistolary period. He alludes in it to one of the Rev. Stewart D. Headlam's Church and Stage parties, which took place always in January, and were a brilliant and picturesque episode in the artistic life of the early nineties. They should be put on record. The customary scene in his beautiful drawing-rooms will remain impressed on the minds of his many grateful guests.

. . .

The Rhymers held one memorable meeting in Mr Herbert Horne's rooms in the Fitzroy settlement. They were then, so to speak, rediscovered and reconstituted, having previously been but a small group of Dublin poets. It was an evening of notabilities. Mr Walter Crane stood with his back to the mantelpiece, deciding, very kindly, on the merits of our effusions. And round Oscar Wilde, not then under a cloud, hovered reverently Lionel Johnson and Ernest Dowson, with others. This must have been in 1891, and I marvelled at the time to notice the fascination which poor Wilde exercised over the otherwise rational. He sat as it were enthroned and surrounded by a deferential circle. Describing the scene from hearsay, my friend Mr Morley Roberts declared that Wilde wore a black shirt front and that Dowson and Johnson, small fairy creatures in white, climbed about upon it. Of the close of this meeting, or of a quite other gathering in my own rooms in January, 1892, the same brilliant weaver of fancies declared that all the people present clasped hands and whirled down the stairs like human catherine wheels, striking sparks as they went on the stone stairs, where to this day hang Professor Image's fine cartoons of Saint Peter and other saints.

BRENNBAUM

Turning to a series of contemporary portraits, Pound begins with the Jew, inheritor of the long tradition of "Horeb, Sinai and the forty years," who cancels his entire heritage and assumes a smooth mask of correctness in order to conform to the age.

*   *   *

In his notes to Friar, Pound remarks that Mr. Nixon (see below) is a "fictitious name for a real person." That Brennbaum "The Impeccable" is also based, at least in part, on a living model seems probable when one thinks of "The Incomparable Max" and becomes certain when one reads in the essay on Gourmont: ". . . there was the 'aesthetic' era during which people 'wrought' as the impeccable Beerbohm has noted. . . ." The model can only have provided the physical details of the portrait, unless Pound was writing under the mistaken impression that the Beerbohm family was Jewish.

MR. NIXON

The literary opportunist, out to make money, is second in the gallery.

*   *   *

In all probability, as Kenner suggests, this portrait is modeled on Arnold Bennett, to whom Pound refers twice in his published letters as an author who frankly declared that his real interest in letters was financial. "The mistake of my life was in beginning in London as if publishers were any different from bucket shops. Arnold Bennett knew his eggs. Whatever his interest in good writing, he never showed the public anything but his AVARICE. Consequently, they adored him." "The respectable and the middle generation, illustrious punks and messers, fakes like Shaw, stew like Wells, nickle cash-register Bennett."

Dr. Dundas stands for the Waugh-Strachey-Gosse type of literary pontiff and editor.

Perhaps it is worth commenting on the appropriateness of Bishop Blougram's friend's using the Pauline "kick against the pricks." (And Pound would hardly have been deaf to the undercurrent of ribaldry here as well.)

X

The dedicated stylist is forced to live in the country, unable to meet the economic pressures of his age and unwilling to yield to them.

*　　*　　*

Kenner suggests Ford Madox Ford as the probable model here, pointing out that for a period Ford lived under precisely these circumstances.

XI

The middle-class woman (as opposed to the stylist's "placid and uneducated mistress") lives entirely by dictated habit, her instincts completely smothered.

XII

Forced to a realization that the contemporary world has no

place for him, Pound castigates the fashionable literary salons of London where poetry and art are used not for themselves but as devices for self-advancement in society. The poet is forced to crown himself with the laurel, and Fleet Street, which once stood for something, is now taken over by the haberdasher.

* * *

Though no individual prototype for "The Lady Valentine" may be intended here, the trisyllable suggests both Lady Otto-line Morrel and Lady Geraldine Otter, neither of whose circles Pound would have found comforting.

"Pierian roses" in the sense of "poetry" derives ultimately from one of Sappho's fragments, and is here a muted echo of "Sappho's barbitos" in the third poem. Sappho's lines are addressed to a woman of no culture who will "have no share in the roses from Pieria." Sappho's flower in the *Anthology* is the rose, and Pieria is traditionally associated with worship of the Muses.

ENVOI (1919)

Leaving the careful quatrains, Pound now sings his own fare-well in a song based on Waller's *Go, Lovely Rose*, which was set to music by Henry Lawes. The poem sounds throughout the suggestion of active passion as earnest against the destruction of Time. The echoes of the long line of English poets from Chaucer down are so varied and interwoven as to make a complete unraveling almost impossible; but the ironic triumph of this lyric in answer to the critical dismissal of Pound in the *Ode* is, for the balance of the entire suite, its most important function.

MAUBERLEY (1920)
"*Vacuous exercet aera morsus.*"

The figure of Hugh Selwyn Mauberley disengages itself for the first time, and always in contrast to the active Odysseus-poet of the first section. Mauberley is characterized as a minor artist, turning from the detailed etching to the profile of Rome's most profligate empress, and the ribald echoes of the *Ode* are taken up in the second stanza. Mauberley is limited, unable to create a tradition of his own ("forge Achaia"), but he has not compromised with the age.

*   *   *

The epigraph, except for the omission of *in*, is a common reading in a number of late manuscripts of Ovid. The reading most frequently given, however, is *Vanos exercet in aera motus*, but for Pound's purposes the image of the mouth snapping emptily in the air is far more effective than simply the vain leaping of the dog Laelaps would be.

Of Messalina, Friar says: "Pound writes the editor that he had in mind a particular portrait, but that he cannot now remember which." Though it is not an essential point for understanding *Mauberley*, perhaps it should be made clear that the only "portraits" of Messalina Pound would have been likely to examine would be those on coins struck during the early years of Claudius' reign. None bearing portraits of Messalina were struck in Rome, but a few were issued in outlying parts of the empire, two in particular from the mint in Caesarea in Cappadocia. Whatever coin Pound saw, either in the British Museum collection or in reproduction, would have had the head in profile. That Mauberley should take his suggestion for "the series of curious heads in medallion" from a portrait of the most licentious woman in Rome is another of the poem's ironies.

I follow Friar in noting that Reinach's *Apollo*, Mauberley's own reference work, speaks of Piero della Francesca as being "cold and impersonal" in his work and refers to his "pale, straight figures." Pisanello, the great Veronese medalist, is one of Pound's favorite artists and plays a role in *The Cantos*.

II

Mauberley, after living for three years in his own illusions, awakens to the realization that love, whose invitation he had not even recognized when it was given, must remain for him only a retrospective possibility.

"THE AGE DEMANDED"

Unable to respond to the age's demands, and unequal to forging his own tradition, Mauberley is gradually driven into himself, his thoughts interrupted twice by an internal vision of tropical islands, and drifts finally into a subjective voyage.

* * *

Mauberley's inability to relate beauty to anything but itself, his finding of the month only "more temperate" because of the existence of beauty, is a distant echo of the Shakespearean overtones of the *Envoi* and is the nearest he ever comes to response. "The glow of porcelain," the "perfect glaze," and the "Minoan undulation" all contribute to the closing *Medallion*.

Although the primary source of Mauberley's tropical vision is Flaubert's *Salammbô*, Homer and possibly Conrad contribute to it. Writing to W. H. D. Rouse in 1935, Pound observed:

Para thina poluphloisboio thalasses: the turn of the wave and the scutter of receding pebbles.

Year's work to get that. Best I have been able to do is cross cut in *Mauberley*, led up to:

...*imaginary*
Audition of the phantasmal sea-(s)urge

which is totally different, and a different movement of the water, and inferior.

That Homer's phrase had been a constant preoccupation with Pound is clear from the sixth poem of *Moeurs Contemporaines* which refers to "the poluphloisboious sea-coast," and then simply quotes the original Greek.

The presence of Conrad is by no means as certain, but *Victory* received some attention in *The Egoist* during this period and the opening description of Heyst's boyhood,

For three years, after leaving school at the age of eighteen, followed almost immediately by

> "I'll drift," Heyst had said to himself deliberately.
> He did not mean intellectually or sentimentally or morally. He meant to drift altogether and literally, body and soul. . . .

may have had an effect on the second poem in the "Mauberley" section, with "For three years, diabolus in the scale," followed shortly by "Drifted . . . drifted precipitate."

IV

Drifting now through the Spice Islands of his revery, Mauberley goes to his death.

*   *   *

The oar inscription is again a direct contrast to the Odysseus theme of the *Ode*, derived from the passage in which Elpenor asks Odysseus to memorialize him. In Pound's own translation, as it occurs in *Canto I*:

> "Heap up mine arms, be tomb by sea-bord, and inscribed:
> "*A man of no fortune, and with a name to come.*
> "And set my oar up, that I swung mid fellows."

MEDALLION

Hugh Selwyn Mauberley's single poem, his one "curious head," the portrait of the singing woman whose song has been answered by the active poet of the *Envoi*, stands as his final monument. He compares her with a portrait by Bernardino Luini (*La Columbina?*), he notes the details of the scene, the wedding-color of her dress, the qualities of her eyes, and is reminded of Venus, not a living goddess but a reproduction in the early pages of Reinach's *Apollo*.

That the foregoing pages are not intended as a "substitute" for *Mauberley* itself is, I hope, clear. And if anyone is so foolish as to think that they can serve as a substitute, he need only turn to the poem itself and read it through.

7 mauberley as node

If it is a truism that any major poem is both a summary of its author's past writing and a prefiguring of his future work, it is at least a truism worth repeating in connection with *Mauberley*. Few poems of similar length can have condensed so stringently the greater part of an individual literary history, and it is a history that deserves brief review before one advances to what is perhaps the most interesting aspect of the poem to the general reader: *Mauberley*'s relation to *The Cantos*.

Mauberley contains in capsule many of Pound's early enthusiasms: his devotion to Browning, his interest in Swinburne and the pre-Raphaelites, his admiration of FitzGerald's *Rubaiyat* as a much-needed transfusion of new blood for the sluggish stream of nineteenth-century English poetry, his early allegiance to Dowson and Lionel Johnson as the most useful poets of the Nineties; and even the Anglo-Saxon studies, which produced his translation of *The Seafarer*, leave a trace in the coined kenning "earth's lid." The sequence reflects Pound's classical interests in its use of Homeric themes and its evocation of Sappho's barbitos and the Pierian roses; the ribaldry of some of the sexual references remind one that Pound's favorites among the Latin poets are Ovid, Propertius, and Catullus. His dissociation of these poets of individual, private strength from the celebrators of public virtue is here, too, in the echoes of Pindar, Horace, and Cicero; and the underlying theme owes much to his appreciation of the Provençal poets, with Dante's *De Vulgari Eloquentia* probably first leading him to the line from the King of Navarre.

The order of contents in *Poems 1918–21* is itself the clearest indication of *Mauberley's* pivotal position. The book opens with *Homage to Sextus Propertius*, which is followed by *Langue d'Oc* and its complement, *Moeurs Contemporaines*, the two units together summarizing Pound's early focus on the Provençal poets and his later interest in Flaubert, Gautier, and Gourmont. *Mauberley* then follows as the last of the book's "Three Portraits," and is followed in turn by the fourth, fifth, sixth, and seventh *Cantos*.

The relationship between Pound's *Homage to Sextus Propertius* and *Hugh Selwyn Mauberley* remains to be investigated. In 1932 Pound wrote to John Drummond:

I wonder how far the Mauberley is merely a translation of the Homage to S. P., for such as couldn't understand the letter?

An endeavour to communicate with a blockheaded epoch.

The Pound of 1932 looking back to the Pound of 1920 may not be an altogether reliable guide, but for the present it is enough to note, as a number of persons have noted before this, that both *Propertius* and *Mauberley* are works of self-justification, concerned with the fate of the artist in an age unsympathetic to his art. But whereas Pound's *Propertius*, that booby-trap for the classicist who is also a pedant, requires for its fullest savor some knowledge of the text on which it is based and depends on two lines,

Go on, to Ascraeus' prescription, the ancient,
                              respected, Wordsworthian:
"A flat field for rushes, grapes grow on the slope."

for its immediate application to the present, *Mauberley* is always pertinent, is fused with Pound's personal emotion, and comments without obliqueness on the contemporary scene. The two works move in quite different patterns, and even if one accepts Pound's judgment of *Mauberley* as a poor-man's *Propertius*, we live, perhaps, in an age of poor men. What is more germane here is that *Propertius* was still so fresh in Pound's mind that it not only produced a rehandling of the general theme but also left detailed traces on *Mauberley*.

The first of these traces is the reference in the *Ode* to Capaneus (a hero of Pound's first named in *The Spirit of Romance*), who is mentioned once by Propertius with precise reference to his destruction, and twice by implication when Evadne is named as a model of the devoted wife.[18] There is little to be gained by insisting on the mention of Evadne and Penelope together here; for Pound's *Ode* is made up of almost standard classic tags.

The opening of *Mauberley*'s third poem shows a further trace of Propertius in an interesting wedding of the Latin elegist's vocabulary and the language of Gautier, Laforgue, and James. In *Homage to Sextus Propertius* Pound had taken Propertius'

> sive illam Cois fulgentem incedere coas,
>   hoc totum e Coe veste volumen erit,

soberly rendered in the Loeb series as "If thou wilt have her walk radiant in silks of Cos, of Coan raiment all this my book shall tell," and turned them into

> If she goes in a gleam of Cos, in a slither of dyed stuff,
>   There is a volume in the matter;

---

[18] Amphiarea tibi non prosint fata quadrigae
aut Capanei magno grata ruini Iovi.   (II, xxxiv, 39–40)

coniugis Euadne miseros elata per ignes
occidit, Argivae fama pudicitiae.   (I, xv, 21–22)

hoc genus infidum nuptarum, hic nulla puella
nec fida Euadne nec pia Penelope.   (III, xiii, 23–24)

and now in *Mauberley* he echoes the passage with

> The tea-rose tea-gown, etc.
> Supplants the mousseline of Cos.

Mauberley's reference to Achaia, standard as it is, may be a Propertian remnant, but the most remarkable echo is the last, found in "*The Age Demanded*":

> For this agility chance found
> Him of all men, unfit
> As the red-beaked steeds of
> The Cytharæan for a chain bit.

The base for this reference to Venus's doves is

> et Veneris dominae volucres, mea turba, columbae
> tingunt Gorgoneo punica rostra lacu;
> (III, iii, 31–32)

which, rather than "and doves, birds of my lady Venus, the birds I love, dipped their red bills in the Gorgon's fount," Pound had rendered

> The small birds of the Cytharean mother,
> their Punic faces dyed in the Gorgon's lake.

Pound had been attacked in the pages of *Poetry* (April, 1919) by William Gardner Hale of the University of Chicago, the first victim of the *Propertius* trap,[19] who took Pound to task for a number of readings, among them the translation of *punica* as "Punic," and suggested that as a translator Pound had nothing left but to commit suicide. The lines in *Mauberley* stand as an ironic reply, possibly brought to mind by a stanza of Gautier's

---

[19] *Poetry*'s publication of an emasculated selection from the poems under a somewhat misleading title contributed to the confusion, which is not yet resolved in certain circles.

Odelette Anacreontique from *Émaux et Camées*,[20] with their thoroughly academic reading of "red-beaked" joined to the non-academic "steeds of the Cytharaean" and the mouth image made vivid by the "chain bit."

If *Mauberley* is a summary *in petto* of the greater part of Pound's work up to this point, it is also a thumbnail outline of many themes in *The Cantos*, though it is not an anticipation strictly speaking, for the first three *Cantos* (later canceled, but parts of them preserved) had appeared in *Poetry* in 1917. Anyone who has mastered the miniature handling of devices and techniques in *Mauberley* is prepared for their larger use in *The Cantos*. This is not to say that *The Cantos* are simply an extension or an expansion of *Mauberley*—it would be more accurate to say that *Mauberley* states a problem that *The Cantos* attempt to solve—but to propose that anyone who can handle the rapid juxtaposition of

> Bent resolutely on wringing lilies from the acorn;
> Capaneus; trout for factitious bait,

on all levels is prepared for *The Cantos*' larger units and has no difficulty in grasping at least some of the larger work's movement.

Quite on the surface, *Mauberley* uses a number of devices found in *The Cantos*. The contrast gained by using Greek itself for the first section of *Mauberley* and the transliterations of Greek for the second prepares one for the variant forms of *The Cantos* and the same play of contrasts. The breaking off of the twelfth poem in *Mauberley* and the coda following the asterisks, the use of the hesitant periods in the second poem of the "Mauberley" section, the suggestive enclosure of "(Orchid)"—all these are part of *The Cantos*' technical surface, where they

---

[20] Et la colombe apprivoisée
Sur ton épaule t'abattra,
Et son bec à pointe rosée
De ton baiser s'enivrera.

become more elaborately developed and culminate in the introduction of Chinese ideographs and a musical score.

More important to other levels of Pound's work is the appearance of an entire group of individuals, already touchstones for Pound when *Mauberley* was written. Anyone at ease with the "*Siena mi fé*" poem has no trouble when he reads

> Prone in that grass, in sleep;
>   et j'entendis des voix: . . .
>
>   wall . . . Strasbourg
> Gallifet led that triple charge . . . Prussians
> and he said
>   it was for the honour of the army.
> And they called him a swashbuckler.
>   I didn't know what it was
> But I thought: This is pretty bloody damn fine.
> And my old nurse, he was a man nurse, and
> He killed a Prussian and he lay in the street
> there in front of our house for three days
> And he stank. . . . . . .

recognizing Victor Plarr's voice (and Pound's misspelling of Galliffet), even without the help of the marginal gloss *Plarris narrations* of the Faber and Faber text (omitted in the New Directions edition). Browning (*Canto II*), Pindar and Catullus and Sappho (*Canto IV*), Henry James (*Canto VII*), Pisanello (*Canto XXVI*) are all here. *The Rubaiyat* announces itself three times, first in *Canto XV* with

>   "Whether in Naishapur or Babylon"
>   I heard in the dream.[21]

Then, much later, in *The Pisan Cantos* (*Canto LXXX*) one comes upon

---

[21] Whether at Naishapur or Babylon
  Whether the cup with sweet or bitter run
    The wine of life keeps oozing drop by drop,
   The leaves of life keep falling one by one.   (Stanza VIII)

> lay there till Rossetti found it remaindered
> at about two pence

and a page or two beyond in the same *Canto* the *Rubaiyat* stanza itself appears as base for the lyric

> Tudor indeed is gone and every rose,
> Blood-red, blanch-white that in the sunset glows
> Cries: "Blood, Blood, Blood!" against the gothic stone
> Of England, as the Howard or Boleyn knows.[22]

Moving on to the larger themes, one can see the relation between the World War poems in *Mauberley* and the more detailed, individualized treatment of the War in *Canto XVI*. The "modern hell" *Cantos* (*XIV* and *XV*) appear as further developments of *Mauberley*'s "liars in public places" and its condemnation of England's rulers and the press with, as in *Mauberley*, a sexual emphasis:

> .....m Episcopus, waving a condom full of black-beetles,
> obstructors of distribution.

It would be absurd to say that the Chinese *Cantos* (*LII–LXI*) are contained in *Mauberley*, but the basis of the general rule of thumb by which, as Kenner has pointed out, Pound evaluates each reign and dynasty through determining whether or not the emperor has fallen into the hands of his palace eunuchs, is present in *Mauberley*'s "Knave or an eunuch / To rule over us." Underlying all *The Cantos* is the usury pattern, which *Mauberley* shows was already the fundamental evil in Pound's mind, "Usury age-old and age-thick" responsible for the "old bitch gone in the teeth," the "botched civilization."

Each of these themes could be commented upon at greater length, but in relation to *Mauberley* they do not deserve quite the

---

[22] Iram indeed is gone with all his Rose
And Jamshyd's Seven ring'd Cup where no one knows,
But still a Ruby kindles in the vine
And many a Garden by the Water blows.   (Stanza V)

emphasis due the chief remaining connection between *Mauberley* and *The Cantos*: the theme of the poet as Odysseus. *Mauberley* opens with this theme and so do *The Cantos*. One of the unifying narrative threads of the first half of *The Cantos* is that of Odysseus, and one can see Hugh Selwyn Mauberley and his subjective revery as part of the movement and feeling of the Lotophagoi passages of *Canto XX*:

> "What gain with Odysseus,
> "They that died in the whirlpool
> "And after many vain labours,
> "Living by stolen meat, chained to the rowingbench,
> "That he should have a great fame
>
>   "And lie by night with the goddess?
> "Their names are not written in bronze
>   "Nor their rowing sticks set with Elpenor's;
> "Nor have they mound by sea-bord.

And, later

> "Nor lay there with the queen's waiting maids,
> "Nor had they Circe to couch-mate, Circe Titania,
> "Nor had they meats of Kalüpso
> "Or her silk skirts brushing their thighs.
> "Give! What were they given?
>
>   Ear-wax.

This narrative line runs from the embarkation of Odysseus (*Canto I*) to his entry into hell for the speech with Tiresias and reaches its climax in *Canto XLVII* with the return of Odysseus-Adonis to take part in the rite of inseminating the earth. Here the Greek refrain is precisely the "Syrian syncopation of Bion's Adonis," with

Τυ Διώνα

TU DIONA

Και Μοῖραι τ'"Αδωνιν

KAI MOIRAI T'ADONIN

used early in the Canto and repeated first in

$$Και\ Μοῖραι\ τ'\ ˝Αδωνιν$$
KAI MOIRAI T'ADONIN

and again in

$$Τυ\ Διώνα,\ Και\ Μοῖραι$$
TU DIONA, KAI MORAI

$$Και\ Μοῖραι\ τ'\ ˝Αδωνιν^{23}$$
KAI MOIRAI T'ADONIN

at the Canto's climax. The references are specifically sexual throughout:

> Hast thou found a nest softer than cunnus
> Or hast thou found better rest
> Hast'ou a deeper planting, doth thy death year
> Bring swifter shoot?
> Hast thou entered more deeply the mountain?

> The light has entered the cave. Io! Io!
> The light has gone down into the cave,
> Splendour on splendour!
> By prong have I entered these hills:
> That the grass grow from my body,
> That I hear the roots speaking together,
> The air is new on my leaf,
> The forked boughs shake with the wind.
> Is Zephyrus more light on the bough, Apeliota
> more light on the almond branch?
> By this door have I entered the hill.
> Falleth,
> Adonis falleth.
> Fruit cometh after.

Here is the very bedrock of *The Cantos*, the creation of order ($τὸ\ καλὸν$ for Pound) out of the formless, the male organ informing the female chaos.

---

[23] The Greek here is an attempt to harmonize three conflicting texts by Pound with Bion's original.

If *Mauberley* offers some keys to the strength of *The Cantos* it also offers clues to their weakness. The disparity between surface complexity and over-simplification of base characteristic of *Mauberley* at certain levels is probably the most revealing of these clues. Though it is not within the limits of this study to determine how the author of *Mauberley* who admired Swinburne and James as fighters against personal oppression came to support a political movement that made such oppression almost a policy, it is nevertheless possible to indicate that at least part of the solution lies in this disparity, which reveals itself most tellingly in Pound's eagerness to discover final answers, in his reliance on judgments that, once formulated, are never revised. How early some of them are set *Mauberley* makes plain. Another part of the solution probably lies in the pleasure Pound took in Gautier's and Flaubert's contempt for "la bêtise moderne."

But if much of this lies outside a study of *Mauberley*, what does not lie outside it is some examination of Pound's method and creative processes. Probably the first thing that needs to be said is that all the slips, the misspellings, the inaccurate quotations should not influence one's judgment of *Mauberley* as a poem. Though they cannot, I think, be equaled in number anywhere else in a work of similar length, they are part of an honorable tradition that includes almost all the illustrious names in English and American literature. What they do indicate is Pound's haste, his eager fastening upon what is at hand and pressing it into service. However imperfect the assimilation may be at times, the result often justifies the method.

Two characteristics of Pound's creative process are particularly conspicuous in his use of the auxiliary materials out of which he shaped *Mauberley*. The first is his eye for the typical, the representative and summarizing word or phrase. "Yeux glauques" is the most prominent example in *Mauberley*, epitomizing as it does certain characteristics of the nineteenth century and including at the same time specific centers in Flaubert, Gautier, and Gourmont. The second characteristic is similar to the first but, I think, quite distinct. It is the catalytic function played in Pound's mind by certain phrases and certain ideas that precipitate and arrange other phrases and ideas about themselves. The most interesting instance of this in *Mauberley* is the way in which the orchid and iris of the Fenollosa notes attract to themselves the entire elaborate pattern of the second "Mauberley" poem.

Although these characteristics are related to Pound's accomplishments as a translator, it is, I think, necessary to insist that they carry their own originality with them. The "tea-rose tea-gown" passage is the result of genuine fusion and is not just a pastiche. "The pure mind / Arose toward Newman as the whiskey warmed" is altogether personal and witty. The "tin wreath" pun is crushingly effective. Eliot's evaluation in 1928 of *Mauberley* as a poem "compact of the experience of a certain man in a certain place at a certain time" that "is also a document of an epoch," "Genuine tragedy and comedy; and . . . in the best sense of Arnold's worn phrase, a 'criticism of life' " does not, in the end, appear disproportionate to *Mauberley*'s qualities.

After the review of some major themes sounded in both *Mauberley* and *The Cantos* and after this brief characterization of some of Pound's qualities, it may be useful to conclude with another relationship between *Mauberley* and *The Cantos*, a quite personal one that, if one admits any connection between a poet and his work, gives to *The Pisan Cantos* a level of individual emotion rarely felt in the earlier sections of the work. Pound, held in a prison enclosure, once again under personal pressure, with almost no books, turns repeatedly to the period of *Mauberley*'s composition and to the years of which *Mauberley* was the culmination. Ford Madox Ford, Yeats, Joyce, and James all appear in *Canto LXXIV*. The *Mauberley* nexus of the pre-Raphaelites, the Nineties, Circe ("so lay men in Circe's swinesty"), and Pisanello leads to direct quotation from *Mauberley* itself and a moving passage from Capaneus, how ironically blasted now, to his Evadne:

> Time is not, Time is the evil, beloved
> Beloved the hours βροδοδάκτυλος
> > as against the half-light of the window
> > with the sea beyond making horizon
> le contre-jour the line of the cameo
> profile "to carve Achaia"
> > a dream passing over the face in the half-light
> > Venere, Cytherea "aut Rhodon"
> > vento ligure, veni
> "Beauty is difficult" sd/ Mr Beardsley.

With the specific announcement of *Mauberley* and the beauty theme, the poem becomes part of the musical variation:

> . . . . cheek bone, by verbal manifestation,
> > her eyes as in "La Nascita"

where it may not be insignificant that Pound returns to the 1920 "manifestation" rather than the later plural, though one cannot put great weight on the single letter. Later in the same canto the note is sounded again with

> for the deification of emperors
> and the medallions
> > to forge Achaia.

In *Canto LXXVI* Gautier is mentioned in a passing reference to "Teofile's bricbrac" and farther in the canto the personal emotion overflows again through one of the insect-images that Kenner has noted may derive from *Physique de l'Amour*:

> As a lone ant from a broken ant-hill
> from the wreckage of Europe, ego scriptor.

The emotion rises again in

> O white-chested martin, God damn it,
> > as no one else will carry a message,
> say to La Cara: amo.

And a few lines later a distant touch of Henry James appears in "gli onesti" to be followed at some distance by Sappho's τίς ἀδικεῖ.

Canto LXXVII refers wittily to Eliot's derivation from *Émaux et Camées* as Pound speaks of

> or Grishkin's photo refound years after
> with the feeling that Mr Eliot may have
> missed something, after all, in composing his vignette periplum,

and in *Canto LXXIX* Henry James and Odysseus appear jointly:

> Which being the case, her holding dear H. J.
> (Mr. James, Henry) literally by the button-
> hole . . .
> In those so consecrated surroundings
> (a garden in the Temple, no less)
> and saying, *for once*, the right thing
> namely: "Cher maître"
> to his checquered waistcoat, the Princess Bariatinsky,
> as the fish-tails said to Odysseus, ἐνὶ Τροίῃ.

Arthur Symons remembers "Verlaine at the Tabarin or Hennique, Flaubert" in *Canto LXXX* to be followed shortly by a reference to "the hair of Circe" and some distance beyond by

> Judith's junk shop
> with Theophile's arm chair
> one cd/live in such an apartment
> seeing the roofs of Paris
> Ça s'appelle une mansarde

with its reminder of *La Mansarde* in *Émaux et Camées*. Yeats, "labouring a sonnet of Ronsard" and "M. Arnold Bennett" lead up to Pound's own lyric message in which he quotes directly from Ronsard:

          Quand vous serez bien vieille
                    remember that I have remembered,
    mia pargoletta,
          and pass on the tradition
    there can be honesty of mind
                    without overwhelming talent.

Though the personal level of "senesco sed amo" and "Down, Derry-down / Oh let an old man rest" is in many ways the most moving part of *The Pisan Cantos*, it cannot provide a basis for the final judgment of the entire work. What it can do, however, is offer a means of entry into the work of a poet who has created about himself an aura of such political and economic emotionalism that some counter-current of feeling seems necessary before one can begin to make anything like a final judgment. Such a judgment lies altogether outside the limits of the present study, but I should be disingenuous if I did not say that any critic's evaluation of *Mauberley* is in all probability a miniature of his evaluation of *The Cantos*, with the single qualification that though the strengths remain constant, the flaws are magnified in the larger work.

hugh selwyn mauberley

(contacts and life)

"vocat aestus in umbram"

Nemesianus Ec. IV.

E. P. ODE POUR L'ELECTION DE SON SEPULCHRE

For three years, out of key with his time,
He strove to resuscitate the dead art
Of poetry; to maintain "the sublime"
In the old sense. Wrong from the start—

No, hardly, but seeing he had been born
In a half savage country, out of date;
Bent resolutely on wringing lilies from the acorn;
Capaneus; trout for factitious bait;

"Ἴδμεν γάρ τοι πάνθ', ὅσ'ἐνὶ Τροίη
Caught in the unstopped ear;
Giving the rocks small lee-way
The chopped seas held him, therefore, that year.

His true Penelope was Flaubert,
He fished by obstinate isles;
Observed the elegance of Circe's hair
Rather than the mottoes on sun-dials.

Unaffected by "the march of events,"
He passed from men's memory in *l'an trentuniesme*
De son eage; the case presents
No adjunct to the Muses' diadem.

II

The age demanded an image
Of its accelerated grimace,
Something for the modern stage,
Not, at any rate, an Attic grace;

Not, not certainly, the obscure reveries
Of the inward gaze;
Better mendacities
Than the classics in paraphrase!

The "age demanded" chiefly a mould in plaster,
Made with no loss of time,
A prose kinema, not, not assuredly, alabaster
Or the "sculpture" of rhyme.

III

The tea-rose tea-gown, etc.
Supplants the mousseline of Cos,
The pianola "replaces"
Sappho's barbitos.

Christ follows Dionysus,
Phallic and ambrosial
Made way for macerations;
Caliban casts out Ariel.

All things are a flowing,
Sage Heracleitus says;
But a tawdry cheapness
Shall outlast our days.

Even the Christian beauty
Defects—after Samothrace;
We see τὸ καλόν
Decreed in the market place.

Faun's flesh is not to us,
Nor the saint's vision.
We have the press for wafer;
Franchise for circumcision.

All men, in law, are equals.
Free of Pisistratus,
We choose a knave or an eunuch
To rule over us.

O bright Apollo,
τίν’ ἄνδρα, τίν’ ἥρωα, τίνα θεόν,
What god, man, or hero
Shall I place a tin wreath upon!

IV

These fought in any case,
and some believing,
>   pro domo, in any case . . .

Some quick to arm,
some for adventure,
some from fear of weakness,
some from fear of censure,
some for love of slaughter, in imagination,
learning later . . .
some in fear, learning love of slaughter;

Died some, pro patria,
>   non "dulce" non "et decor" . . .
walked eye-deep in hell
believing in old men's lies, then unbelieving
came home, home to a lie,
home to many deceits,
home to old lies and new infamy;
usury age-old and age-thick
and liars in public places.

Daring as never before, wastage as never before.
Young blood and high blood,
fair cheeks, and fine bodies;

fortitude as never before

frankness as never before,
disillusions as never told in the old days,
hysterias, trench confessions,
laughter out of dead bellies.

V

There died a myriad,
And of the best, among them,
For an old bitch gone in the teeth,
For a botched civilization,

Charm, smiling at the good mouth,
Quick eyes gone under earth's lid,

For two gross of broken statues,
For a few thousand battered books.

YEUX GLAUQUES

Gladstone was still respected,
When John Ruskin produced
"Kings' Treasuries"; Swinburne
And Rossetti still abused.

Fœtid Buchanan lifted up his voice
When that faun's head of hers
Became a pastime for
Painters and adulterers.

The Burne-Jones cartons
Have preserved her eyes;
Still, at the Tate, they teach
Cophetua to rhapsodize;

Thin like brook-water,
With a vacant gaze.
The English Rubaiyat was still-born
In those days.

The thin, clear gaze, the same
Still darts out faunlike from the half-ruin'd
    face,
Questing and passive. . . .
"Ah, poor Jenny's case" . . .

Bewildered that a world
Shows no surprise
At her last maquero's
Adulteries.

"*SIENA MI FE'; DISFECEMI MAREMMA*"

Among the pickled fœtuses and bottled bones,
Engaged in perfecting the catalogue,
I found the last scion of the
Senatorial families of Strasbourg, Monsieur Verog.

For two hours he talked of Galliffet;
Of Dowson; of the Rhymers' Club;
Told me how Johnson (Lionel) died
By falling from a high stool in a pub . . .

But showed no trace of alcohol
At the autopsy, privately performed—
Tissue preserved—the pure mind
Arose toward Newman as the whiskey warmed.

Dowson found harlots cheaper than hotels;
Headlam for uplift; Image impartially imbued
With raptures for Bacchus, Terpsichore and the
          Church.
So spoke the author of "The Dorian Mood,"

M. Verog, out of step with the decade,
Detached from his contemporaries,
Neglected by the young,
Because of these reveries.

BRENNBAUM

The skylike limpid eyes,
The circular infant's face,
The stiffness from spats to collar
Never relaxing into grace;

The heavy memories of Horeb, Sinai
        and the forty years,
Showed only when the daylight fell
Level across the face
Of Brennbaum "The Impeccable."

MR. NIXON

In the cream gilded cabin of his steam yacht
Mr. Nixon advised me kindly, to advance with fewer
Dangers of delay. "Consider
        "Carefully the reviewer.

"I was as poor as you are;
"When I began I got, of course,
"Advance on royalties, fifty at first," said Mr. Nixon,
"Follow me, and take a column,
"Even if you have to work free.

"Butter reviewers. From fifty to three hundred
"I rose in eighteen months;
"The hardest nut I had to crack
"Was Dr. Dundas.

"I never mentioned a man but with the view
"Of selling my own works.
"The tip's a good one, as for literature
"It gives no man a sinecure.

"And no one knows, at sight, a masterpiece.
"And give up verse, my boy,
"There's nothing in it."

* * * *

Likewise a friend of Blougram's once advised me:
Don't kick against the pricks,
Accept opinion. The "Nineties" tried your game
And died, there's nothing in it.

X

Beneath the sagging roof
The stylist has taken shelter,
Unpaid, uncelebrated,
At last from the world's welter

Nature receives him;
With a placid and uneducated mistress
He exercises his talents
And the soil meets his distress.

The haven from sophistications and
        contentions
Leaks through its thatch;
He offers succulent cooking;
The door has a creaking latch.

XI

"Conservatrix of Milésien"
Habits of mind and feeling,
Possibly. But in Ealing
With the most bank-clerkly of Englishmen?

No, "Milesian" is an exaggeration.
No instinct has survived in her
Older than those her grandmother
Told her would fit her station.

XII

"Daphne with her thighs in bark
"Stretches toward me her leafy hands,"—
Subjectively. In the stuffed-satin
        drawing-room
I await The Lady Valentine's commands,

Knowing my coat has never been
Of precisely the fashion
To stimulate, in her,
A durable passion;

Doubtful, somewhat, of the value
Of well-gowned approbation
Of literary effort,
But never of The Lady Valentine's vocation:

Poetry, her border of ideas,
The edge, uncertain, but a means of blending
With other strata
Where the lower and higher have ending;

A hook to catch the Lady Jane's attention,
A modulation toward the theatre,
Also, in the case of revolution,
A possible friend and comforter.

*   *   *   *

Conduct, on the other hand, the soul
"Which the highest cultures have
    nourished"
To Fleet St. where
Dr. Johnson flourished;

Beside this thoroughfare
The sale of half-hose has
Long since superseded the cultivation
Of Pierian roses.

ENVOI (1919)

Go, dumb-born book,
Tell her that sang me once that song of Lawes:
Hadst thou but song
As thou hast subjects known,
Then were there cause in thee that should condone
Even my faults that heavy upon me lie,
And build her glories their longevity.

Tell her that sheds
Such treasure in the air,
Recking naught else but that her graces give
Life to the moment,
I would bid them live
As roses might, in magic amber laid,
Red overwrought with orange and all made
One substance and one colour
Braving time.

Tell her that goes
With song upon her lips
But sings not out the song, nor knows
The maker of it, some other mouth,

May be as fair as hers,
Might, in new ages, gain her worshippers,
When our two dusts with Waller's shall be laid,
Siftings on siftings in oblivion,
Till change hath broken down
All things save Beauty alone.

MAUBERLEY (*1920*)

"Vacuos exercet in aera morsus."

Turned from the "eau-forte
Par Jacquemart"
To the strait head
Of Messalina:

"His true Penelope
Was Flaubert,"
And his tool
The engraver's.

Firmness,
Not the full smile,
His art, but an art
In profile;

Colourless
Pier Francesca,
Pisanello lacking the skill
To forge Achaia.

II

"Qu'est ce qu'ils savent de l'amour, et qu'est ce qu'ils peuvent
comprendre?
S'ils ne comprennent pas la poésie, s'ils ne sentent pas la musique,

qu'est ce qu'ils peuvent comprendre de cette passion en comparaison avec laquelle la rose est grossière et le parfum des violettes un tonnerre?" CAID ALI

For three years, diabolus in the scale,
He drank ambrosia
All passes, ANANGKE prevails,
Came end, at last, to that Arcadia.

He had moved amid her phantasmagoria,
Amid her galaxies,
NUKTOS AGALMA

* * * *

Drifted . . . drifted precipitate,
Asking time to be rid of . . .
Of his bewilderment; to designate
His new found orchid. . . .

To be certain . . . certain . . .
(Amid ærial flowers) . . . time for
        arrangements—
Drifted on
To the final estrangement;

Unable in the supervening blankness
To sift TO AGATHON from the chaff
Until he found his sieve . . .
Ultimately, his seismograph:

—Given that is his "fundamental passion,"
This urge to convey the relation
Of eye-lid and cheek-bone
By verbal manifestation;

To present the series
Of curious heads in medallion—

He had passed, inconscient, full gaze,
The wide-banded irides
And botticellian sprays implied
In their diastasis;

Which anæsthesis, noted a year late,
And weighed, revealed his great affect,
(Orchid), mandate
Of Eros, a retrospect.

*　*　*　*

Mouths biting empty air,
The still stone dogs,
Caught in metamorphosis, were
Left him as epilogues.

"THE AGE DEMANDED"
Vide Poem II, Page 119

For this agility chance found
Him of all men, unfit
As the red-beaked steeds of
The Cytheræan for a chain bit.

The glow of porcelain
Brought no reforming sense
To his perception
Of the social inconsequence.

Thus, if her colour
Came against his gaze,
Tempered as if
It were through a perfect glaze

He made no immediate application
Of this to relation of the state

To the individual, the month was
    more temperate
Because this beauty had been.

      The coral isle, the lion-coloured sand
      Burst in upon the porcelain revery:
      Impetuous troubling
      Of his imagery.

Mildness, amid the neo-Nietzschean clatter,
His sense of graduations,
Quite out of place amid
Resistance to current exacerbations,

Invitation, mere invitation to perceptivity
Gradually led him to the isolation
Which these presents place
Under a more tolerant, perhaps, examination.

By constant elimination
The manifest universe
Yielded an armour
Against utter consternation,

A Minoan undulation,
Seen, we admit, amid ambrosial circumstances
Strengthened him against
The discouraging doctrine of chances,

And his desire for survival,
Faint in the most strenuous moods,
Became an Olympian *apathein*
In the presence of selected perceptions.

A pale gold, in the aforesaid pattern,
The unexpected palms
Destroying, certainly, the artist's urge,
Left him delighted with the imaginary
Audition of the phantasmal sea-surge,

Incapable of the least utterance or com-
    position,
Emendation, conservation of the "better
    tradition,"
Refinement of medium, elimination of
    superfluities,
August attraction or concentration.

Nothing, in brief, but maudlin confession,
Irresponse to human aggression,
Amid the precipitation, down-float
Of insubstantial manna,
Lifting the faint susurrus
Of his subjective hosannah.

Ultimate affronts to
Human redundancies;

Non-esteem of self-styled "his betters"
Leading, as he well knew,
To his final
Exclusion from the world of letters.

IV

Scattered Moluccas
Not knowing, day to day,
The first day's end, in the next noon;
The placid water
Unbroken by the Simoon;

Thick foliage
Placid beneath warm suns,
Tawn fore-shores
Washed in the cobalt of oblivions;

Or through dawn-mist
The grey and rose

Of the juridical
Flamingoes;

A consciousness disjunct,
Being but this overblotted
Series
Of intermittences;

Coracle of Pacific voyages,
The unforecasted beach;
Then on an oar
Read this:

"I was
"And I no more exist;
"Here drifted
"An hedonist."

MEDALLION

Luini in porcelain!
The grand piano
Utters a profane
Protest with her clear soprano.

The sleek head emerges
From the gold-yellow frock
As Anadyomene in the opening
Pages of Reinach.

Honey-red, closing the face-oval,
A basket-work of braids which seem as
    if they were
Spun in King Minos' hall
From metal, or intractable amber;

The face-oval beneath the glaze,
Bright in its suave bounding-line, as,
Beneath half-watt rays,
The eyes turn topaz.

index